MASTER MENTORS

VOLUME 2

SCOTT JEFFREY MILLER

MASTER MENTORS

VOLUME 2

30 TRANSFORMATIVE INSIGHTS FROM OUR GREATEST MINDS

HarperCollins
Leadership

AN IMPRINT OF HarperCollins

Published by HarperCollins Leadership, an imprint of HarperCollins Focus LLC.

Any internet addresses, phone numbers, or company or product information printed in this book are offered as a resource and are not intended in any way to be or to imply an endorsement by HarperCollins Leadership, nor does Harper-Collins Leadership vouch for the existence, content, or services of these sites, phone numbers, companies, or products beyond the life of this book.

ISBN 978-1-4002-3891-0 (eBook)
ISBN 978-1-4002-3890-3 (TP)

Library of Congress Cataloging-in-Publication Data
Library of Congress Cataloging-in-Publication application has been submitted.

Printed in the United States of America
22 23 24 25 26 LSC 10 9 8 7 6 5 4 3 2 1

TABLE OF CONTENTS

(Continued on following page.)

INTRODUCTION

With some bravado, I declared in *Master Mentors Volume 1* that I would be writing *Master Mentors Volume 2* and beyond. And while everyone has a right to sit down and author a book, getting it published by a reputable publisher is not a right but a privilege. It only happens if an editor and their team choose to invest in your work and have the confidence your book will be well received and actually sell (and sell a lot). Yes, you can self-publish, and I wish anyone exploring that route great success as they navigate the inevitable challenges that follow. *Caveat emptor!*

Publishing is a tough business—if a book doesn't sell well, the author rarely gets a second chance. The fact that you're reading the introduction to *Master Mentors Volume 2* should tell you *Volume 1* sold very well, but more importantly, confirmed that large numbers of readers benefited from a collection of Transformational Insights vetted through my numerous interviews on *FranklinCovey On Leadership with Scott Miller* podcast. Since the publishing of the first book in this series, I've been privileged to speak to nearly a hundred live in-person or virtual audiences and found increasing validation that the power of just one Transformational Insight can be life changing, let alone thirty! *Master Mentors Volume 1* has since been translated into many foreign languages, finding continued relevance to readers around the globe.

I think much of this momentum stems from the fact that our successes, personally and professionally, are often because of the mentors we've had who have helped us navigate the obstacles and opportunities that pop up along our unique life journeys. Sometimes we have a formal relationship with such mentors in which our roles are clearly defined, and there's a distinct beginning and end. More frequently, we experience mentors by what they say, the experiences they share, how they behave, and what they create. Which means the most impactful mentors are often at arm's length—an author whose book we absorb, a podcaster whose episodes we devour, a radio host, a keynote speaker, a historical figure, or someone in the public eye. However we draw upon their wisdom, we admire them and model our lives after them. It seems to me such informal mentorship is increasingly the case if we delve into those whom we strive to use as models in our lives.

It certainly is for me.

Case in point: Bruce Williams, the most influential mentor in my life. I've never met Bruce, and he never knew me. When I was growing up in Central Florida in the eighties, talk radio was just beginning. (If you're of a certain generation, a "radio" is a little box with turn dials and speakers that often doubled as our clocks, alarms, and in some decadent cases, our answering machines. Mind-blowing, I know!)

Beginning in 1981, a small business entrepreneur named Bruce Williams hosted a three-hour call-in radio program originally titled *Talknet*, later renamed *The Bruce Williams Show*. I was twelve years old, and for over a decade, five nights a week for three solid hours, I would be captivated, listening to him dispense wisdom ranging from buying a home or opening a business to creating a will and investing an inheritance. Think Dave Ramsey meets *Shark Tank* meets Dr. Phil. Other kids my age were more likely listening to ABBA, Styx, and Devo, while yours truly absorbed fifteen hours a week of *The Bruce Williams Show*. Perhaps I was the inspiration for Alex P. Keaton and didn't even know it. (Google it.)

Over the years, I listened to thousands of Bruce's episodes as guests shared their business/legal/family/educational challenges and Bruce advised them on their options and how he thought they should proceed. It was the single most formative educational experience of my life. Years later, I find Bruce remains the most influential mentor in my life—more than any relative, leader, priest, or professor. I learned about incorporating a business, all the types of insurances you needed and didn't, how to secure a mortgage, when to use an attorney (and when not to), and a seemingly endless set of life scenarios, many of which, if not all, I've come to face in the 40+ years since I first started being mentored by my friend Bruce.

I never met Bruce Williams or had a conversation with him. He passed away in 2019.

And yet he was absolutely my mentor. A Master Mentor, to be more precise.

My hope in authoring this book is to present such Master Mentors to you, and invite you to enter a similar type of relationship with any or all of the thirty individuals I've featured (make that sixty if you've not read *Volume 1*). If the Transformational Insights from the people I highlight resonate with you, take another step to learn more about them. Buy and read their books. Follow their blogs or subscribe to their newsletters. Connect with them on social media and send them an email or message. I know them all, most very well, and they'd love to hear from you. Because just like you and me, they were mentored by someone, likely many, who challenged them to pay it forward in some way.

I am very proud of this volume and the mentors I've featured here. As I mentioned earlier, the first criteria for being included in the Master Mentors series is that they needed to appear as a guest on *FranklinCovey's On Leadership with Scott Miller* podcast, now the world's largest weekly leadership podcast. Second, they needed to share an insight I deemed "transformational" and then agree to be featured in the book. It is no small task to corral thirty famed leaders from around the world. But to each of them I am grateful for their collaboration and willingness to be featured here. Thanks to them, this volume includes some life-changing stories and insights:

- Zafar Masud, a relatable business leader from Pakistan until the commercial plane he was in crashed, killing everyone on board except him and one other. Now he teaches us to find our purpose and contribution.

- Bobby Herrera, entrepreneur and author of *The Gift of Struggle*. I dare you to make it through this chapter without tearing or choking up and committing to making others feel seen.

- Sean Covey, an author whose books have sold over 10 million copies and who reminds us of the subtle but profound differences between self-worth, self-esteem, and self-confidence.

- Tiffany Aliche, the renowned financial expert and author of *Get Good with Money*. Surprise . . . this Master Mentor teaches us insights far more valuable than how to improve our credit score, like how to build and sustain an enduring brand.

- Turia Pitt, someone living a normal life just like you and me. Until she wasn't. Burned in a horrific fire in Australia, Turia teaches us the life-altering humility associated with being willing to ask for and accept help.

- Patrick Bet-David, the author of *Your Next Five Moves*, is Persian by birth and Californian by luck. Patrick's Transformational Insight has the power not only to change your current mindset, but your entire professional trajectory.

- Ed Mylett, my favorite interview in nearly 250 episodes. You will laugh. You will cry. You will never forget reading this chapter and Ed's hilariously relatable story about headlights and the power of Velcro. Be warned, you're likely to fall in love with Ed Mylett!

And that's just a sample. There are twenty-four more Master Mentors in *Volume 2*, each with a Transformational Insight that may be just the thing to change your life, get you unstuck, shift your paradigm, or inspire you to take on that next great thing in your life. So enjoy the 30 new Master Mentors. And while you're at it, maybe read or reread *Volume 1*. Because *Volume 3* will be here sooner than you can make it through the archived episodes of *The Bruce Williams Show*.

ZAFAR MASUD

FRANKLINCOVEY
ONLEADERSHIP
WITH SCOTT MILLER

EPISODE 144

ZAFAR MASUD
WHAT'S NEXT?

On May 22, 2020, PIA Flight 8303 bounced off the runway in Karachi, Pakistan, its landing gear undeployed. Flames erupted under the damaged engines as they roared back to life, struggling to provide adequate lift. For Zafar Masud, sitting in seat 1C, the next few minutes would have life-altering consequences.

The fifty-year-old CEO of the Bank of Punjab had boarded what was one of the first flights after officials had reinstated global air travel following the early pandemic hiatus. Zafar was at the peak of his professional career, helping to navigate the onset of COVID-19 and the massive changes affecting hundreds of his employees. He'd arrived early enough to the airport to switch his seat from the window to the aisle, as was his preference. Before long, the Airbus A320 left the Iqbal International Airport with ninety-one passengers and eight crew members aboard.

Zafar had settled into his seat in the forward cabin. The short flight from Lahore to Karachi should have been routine. But on its final approach an hour and a half later, the pilots failed to lower the landing gear. The aircraft bounced three times, the engines now critically damaged.

From his seat in the first row, Zafar could clearly recognize panic in the flight attendants' eyes. The aircraft climbed and began to circle, but there was a sudden jerk that caused the cockpit door to fly open. From his vantage point, Zafar could see into the plane's cabin. And through the cockpit windows, he saw they were nosediving.

As Zafar recounted to me in his remarkable *On Leadership* interview, he discovered in that harrowing moment a sense of peace as his life opened up to him "like a canvas." If it was his time to go, he had no regrets about how he'd conducted his life.

The airplane tragically fell short of the runway and crashed into a residential area. Incredibly, Zafar's seat broke free from the aircraft, and beyond all logic and possibility, he landed upright on the roof of a building—unconscious but still belted in his seat. He then slid down the roof, flying off the edge and miraculously landing—again, upright—on a parked car's hood. The impact blew out the windshield of the car, which happened to be occupied by two local residents on their way to work that morning. Completely disoriented, the car's occupants exited their vehicle only to realize there was a man sitting in a plane seat on the front of their car, alive! That Zafar has no memory of this is a small mercy amid such a tremendous tragedy.

The frenzy of the crash was all-consuming to those in the area as fire quickly closed in on Zafar and others in the densely occupied Karachi neighborhood. Thankfully, a gate (later described as "always being locked") was open. Zafar was carried to a waiting ambulance and taken to a hospital, where his long recovery began. Tragically, all but two onboard perished in this unspeakable horror, for which we can only wish their surviving family and friends some modicum of peace in their memory. Additionally, the carnage of this crash took many lives on the ground as well, and we honor their lives and legacies.

Many thought leaders describe their moments of epiphany as being like insights falling from the heavens—Zafar's was far too literal. And it came at great personal cost to himself and those affected by the tragedy that day.

So, what is to be learned from such a tragedy?

What do you do after you've survived a commercial plane crash, coping not only with your own grief, but with a deep and pervasive sense of survivor's guilt over being one of only two who survived? How do you reconcile the incomprehensible chain of events that had to occur to survive such an ordeal?

And what do you do next? What do you do with a second chance?

After nearly two years of physical, mental, and emotional recovery, Zafar shared his Transformational Insight during his *On Leadership* interview: a renewed focus on his family and faith, but also a measurably greater sense of empathy in both his personal and professional life.

Although Zafar had developed an empathetic style of leadership during his career, he'd been "tentative" about it. But after the love and support he received during his recovery, it became clear to him that a human-centered approach mattered most going forward. When he eventually returned to his duties as CEO of the Bank of Punjab, he oriented his entire leadership approach around a level of caring and compassion that builds lasting connections. Zafar calls this "management by empathy," and he is now deeply committed to sharing these principles with other leaders around the world.

Which begs the question: what really matters to you moving forward?

Frankly, I don't think we ask this question enough. That's why I've opened the book with it and why I'm challenging you to gain clarity on this first Transformational Insight: What's Next for you? Because this is personal to you. Perhaps more profoundly, will it take surviving a plane crash for you to get clarity on What's

Next? What will your metaphorical plane crash uncover as your key values?

We might be quick to say we value our families; health (physical, mental, emotional, spiritual); financial security; appreciating simple, daily joy; or even forging a grand and lasting legacy. Or we might prioritize just surviving another day.

Until you know what's most important to you, you can't possibly know what to do next. Not authentically, at least. Only after you're clear about the *What* can you proceed to the *What's Next*.

So, although few of us will face or survive a life-altering tragedy like Zafar, we can heed his example to think deeply about how we live next. We can imagine a "do-over," a chance to clarify and reset our most treasured priorities. And then we can ask ourselves, *What's Next?*

Like many of our *On Leadership* listeners and viewers, I couldn't stop thinking about Zafar's story and insights. Then, shortly after the interview, my oldest son, Thatcher, was working on a sixth-grade writing assignment to identify our family traditions. His answer went something like this:

We go to church on Sundays. After church, we go to lunch. We also watch movies.

I wanted to throw up. Those weren't family traditions—it was a list of activities. Traditions take us deeper. They create powerful memories, provoke positive emotions, and engender meaning. We can pass traditions from one generation to the next, as they require planning and forethought. Activities need only a moment of spontaneity and a willing participant or two. My family's life was full of activities but bereft of traditions—something I valued greatly from my upbringing—and the clock was ticking. If I didn't make a change, they'd soon be adults who would only recall a few vague memories about Sunday lunch. They'd remember life with Mom and Dad as go-go-go, one activity to the next—not creating meaning and memories through traditions—and as a father, that felt absolutely devastating to me.

I recently had the privilege of interviewing the famed author Deepak Chopra, who reminded me that most of us fall into the trap of being Human Doings as opposed to Human Beings. In that moment with Deepak, I realized I was very much caught up in the "doings" of life, known to my son as activities. And I needed to pivot to the "beings" of life, what I'll call traditions. Perhaps it's a small nuance to you, but I can now clearly see a difference.

Insert expletive at that particular realization.

Okay, not a life-and-death plane crash, but a hard landing on the runway of the soul, nonetheless.

So, What's Next for me?

With some contemplation and many conversations (arguments) with my wife, Stephanie, we made a big change. We began a search for a family cabin. Not one of those luxury cabins adorned with high ceilings, antler light fixtures, bearskin rugs, and the latest in gourmet kitchen appliances and other amenities. More of a turn-of-the-twentieth-century-probably-owned-by-an-unsuccessful-panhandler-fixer-upper kind of cabin. But I'd identified my *What*—and now I needed to address the *What's Next*. Weekends playing on a zip-line. Outdoor movies and BBQs that last late into the night. Trapping fireflies (yes, there are fireflies in Utah if you look hard enough) in a glass jar. Holidays with family and friends. Hikes, firepits, and logs on the fire. Games, laughing, and probably a good dose of fighting and wrestling until someone gets hurt, cries, or curses. A technology-free zone ripe for building traditions that can be handed down generation after generation.

When my boys are adults—or even the next time they write about family traditions for school—I'm confident they'll have a more meaningful treasure trove to draw from. I'll update you on the progress in *Master Mentors Volume 3*. If I've resorted to pan-handling at my mountain cabin to pay for it all, at least I'm clear on what matters most and even clearer on *What's Next*.

Do yourself a favor and answer this Transformational Insight for yourself. For me, it started a chain of events I couldn't have fathomed but now wholeheartedly embrace. I also strongly encourage you to watch the *On Leadership* interview with Zafar (see the QR code below). Listening and connecting with him on a personal level can help you clarify your *What* so you can meaningfully and authentically answer your *What's Next?* For me, it was transforming family activities into memorable traditions based on a new definition of what I valued.

· · ·

THE TRANSFORMATIONAL INSIGHT

Until you know what's most important to you—what you value—you can't possibly know what to do next. Don't wait for a near-death experience—you can reflect on these profound questions today.

THE QUESTION

What matters most to you?

Once you've defined that, ask: *What's Next?* What can you do today to live in alignment with your values?

BOBBY HERRERA

FRANKLINCOVEY
ONLEADERSHIP
WITH SCOTT MILLER

EPISODE 133

BOBBY HERRERA
BE A TRANSITION FIGURE

In *Master Mentors Volume 1*, only two of the thirty chapters contained direct transcripts from the actual *On Leadership* podcast interview with the featured mentor: Kim Scott, the author of *Radical Candor*, and Trent Shelton, the former NFL player and author of several bestselling books, including *The Greatest You*. Their own narrative was too powerful to leave to my interpretation. The same is true for Bobby Herrera, the entrepreneur and author of *The Gift of Struggle*. I've read thousands of nonfiction books (I've only read four fiction books outside of required school reading, and *Beowulf* cured me of a love of fiction). I certainly have my favorites (*Zoom* by Istvan Banyai is my all-time #1) but I also have a list of books that contained a story so memorable that I couldn't stop thinking about them, sometimes decades later. *The Gift of Struggle* is one such book. It's the opening story in particular that has profoundly impacted me and is the transformational insight for this chapter: Be a Transition Figure—a concept popularized by Dr. Stephen R. Covey.

Here's the transcript from my podcast interview with Bobby—only slightly edited for reader clarity:

SCOTT: Without question, the opening of your book is one of the most profound that I've read; you call it "the bus story," and I'd like you to take your time and re-create it for our viewers and listeners and also share why it's been so instrumental to your own ongoing leadership style.

BOBBY: When I was seventeen, my brother Ed and I were on a return trip home from a basketball game. And along the way, we stopped for dinner and we were excited as we were celebrating a big win. As we were approaching our stop, I started getting this big pit in my stomach because I knew that the excitement was going to end for me. When the team stopped for dinner at a local restaurant, everybody unloaded off the bus, except for me and my brother Ed. You know, at that point in our family story, we didn't have the means to play sports and go out for dinner. As I mentioned, I'm one of thirteen kids and struggle had been the only consistent theme in our family's story. And so I was very accustomed to staying on that bus. When the rest of the team would get off for dinner, my mom would pack us our dinner and it's just the way things were for us.

Well, a few moments after the team unloaded, one of the dads to the other players steps onboard the bus. And as he's walking toward the back, he teased me a little bit because Ed had outscored me that night. And then he said something to me that I will always remember:

"Bobby, it would make me very happy if you and Ed would allow me to buy you dinner so that you can join the rest of the team. Nobody else has to know. All you have to do to thank me is do the same thing for another great kid in the future."

And to this day, Scott, I can barely tell the story without goose bumps on my arm, and it's hard for me to explain the wave of gratitude that I had at that moment. And, you know, before I could even acknowledge his question, I was getting up out of my seat, and I remember stepping off the bus that evening. And I had no idea what I was going to do with my life. You know, I'm seventeen, I can't see three feet in front of my face. All I knew is that perhaps a year from then I had a desire to raise my hand and join the military. But outside of that, I was clueless. But I vividly recall when I stepped off that bus, although I had no idea what I was going to do, I knew I would somehow, some way, figure out how to create something that would allow me to pay forward that kind act to other kids like me who were born on the wrong side of the opportunity divide. And that moment helped me reframe my story and you know, I mentioned at the beginning, one of the biggest things that I didn't think I was going to be able to do is what I call "check the ultimate box."

Will my story matter? And that moment, that kind act . . . it changed many, many things for me. But the one I'm most grateful for is that it gave me hope, hope that I didn't have at that point in my life that I, too, could do something someday that would allow me to check that box. And if I did something to pay forward that kind act, it would give me meaning. And that moment that evening, it just transformed my life and I often reflect back on that moment, Scott. It's packed with so many lessons.

However, there's an interesting backstory that I think is important to share. You know, the gentleman that stepped on board the bus. His name is Harry Teague and Harry was a very successful businessman in the community. And the narrative that I told myself was that, you know, people like him, they don't see kids like me. And with one kind act, not only did he teach me that I was wrong, but he taught me that one of the single most important parts of leadership is seeing and encouraging potential. That was the very first time in my life that I felt seen. And it just changed everything for me.

Allow me to pause here by interjecting a story of my own.

My father is eighty-five and likely coming down life's home stretch (although his mother lived into her early nineties, so he's still feeling pretty confident). When my father was ten, his father died from a long bout of cancer (circa 1945). His mother was widowed with twin sons, my father Kenneth and his fraternal twin brother Kermit. Yes, *Kermit* . . . as if Kyle, Keith, or Kevin weren't even options. But I digress.

That's a rough hand to be dealt at the end of World War II in nowhere, Minnesota. But that was the beginning of an uphill road for my father's mom, Agnes Miller. Several years later, Kermit, like millions of Americans, caught polio in high school. Soon after, someone from the Knights of Columbus, a Catholic service organization, showed up unannounced and offered to fund the cost of an iron lung for Kermit. As I understand it, polio was wildly contagious and every parent's worst fear for their family. For those who survived, impacts could include paralysis and major respiratory compromise requiring thousands of victims to spend hours, days, and even months in an iron lung (also known as a negative pressure ventilator or NPV). Not exactly in the budget for a widow working as what was commonly called a school "lunchroom lady."

My grandmother, a devout Catholic, declined their help and told them she could afford the treatment for her son, but that the Protestant neighbors couldn't and they should go next door. I mention their religious affiliations as this was an era when it was common for the Catholic and Protestant kids to walk on different sides of the street to and from school. Think Belfast, Northern Ireland, without the guns and bombs.

Let me be clear that Agnes Miller no doubt could have used the funds offered by her own church's service organization (perhaps even desperately) but declined them to help someone else. Despite spending almost a year in an iron lung funded by his mother, Kermit eventually succumbed to the disease and passed in his late twenties.

I don't believe Agnes Miller was being a martyr, but when I heard this story in my early thirties—while she was still alive—it fundamentally changed me. Like Harry Teague changed Bobby Herrera. Harry was Bobby's Transition Figure in life. Agnes Miller was mine.

From me, a Transition Figure is someone in your life who does just that—they impact you so profoundly that you transition into a different kind of person. My grandmother's selflessness, in a time of crippling fear and unspeakable trauma, left an indelible imprint on my own thinking and, hopefully, my ongoing actions. I hope my legacy as a result is one of abundance and generosity and that I, too, might be someone's Transition Figure.

There's a final twist to Bobby's story. Fast-forward about thirty years from the night on the bus with the high school basketball team.

SCOTT: Bobby, I'm emotional listening to your story. I don't want to seem naive that this is the first time I've heard a story of struggle—we all have different struggles in our lives. I think we could spend the whole podcast talking about the lessons from that story. Take it a step further, because I think you mentioned in your book that you reconnected with this gentleman some years later. Tell us how that went and what his response was.

BOBBY: I did and I do share that in the book. I think a couple of other important points the bus story also carries is one of my biggest leadership mistakes. When I started my organization, Populus Group, in 2002, that moment it was raging like an inferno inside of me, and it was my invisible force driving me and I wanted to bring that bus story to life. The big mistake that I made was nobody knew that story. Of course, my brother knew because he'd been on the bus. My wife knew. Outside of them I didn't share it. I didn't have the courage. It was a vulnerable moment for me, and for ten years, I kept that story to myself, and people could feel my intensity. They knew I wanted to build something special and unique, and that I genuinely cared for what I was building, but to them, I was just another intense entrepreneur. And when I finally changed my narrative and developed the courage to share the story, I often say that it helped me begin the transformation of my company to a community, and we've been building on it ever since. Well, fast-forward about four years from the time that I shared that story with my community, and one summer day, I just picked up the phone and I called Mr. Teague and I told him the bus story. He indeed remembered coming on board the bus.

I told him the impact that it had on me and everything I'd been doing to pay forward that kind of work, some of the fortunate things I've been able to do. And it was a very special moment for us. And, you know, a few days later, I get a note from Harry, and in his note, he says, "You know, Bobby, thank you for calling me. Thank you for sharing the bus story. I don't mind sharing the many tears that I shed during and after that call. You made me feel like my life had mattered."

I treasure that note. I'm so grateful that I reached out to him, and last year when I launched *The Gift of Struggle*, I had a big speaking engagement for the launch in Detroit and I didn't tell a soul that I was going to fly Mr. Teague and his wife in, and I did something I'd been waiting thirty-three years to do. I hadn't seen him since I left for the military, and my brother and I bought he and his wife a meal—a lot better than the cheeseburger he bought me. It was a very special day, and at the end of my storytelling session that night, I introduced Mr. Teague to a wonderful crowd there and he got a raging standing ovation. It was a special moment. I wanted him to feel the impact he had made.

SCOTT: Bobby, thank you for your vulnerability. I think one of the reasons why I invited you on is because this is the ultimate manifestation of what Dr. Stephen R. Covey popularized as being a Transition Figure in someone else's life. He talked and wrote and spoke frequently about how, as leaders, we have the remarkable ability to influence people's lives. Sometimes what might seem to be the smallest experience can really have an incalculable impact. You really bring to life this idea of being a Transition Figure. What I'd like to do for a moment is to remind everybody that you never know when you are perhaps putting an indelible imprint on someone. What advice would you offer on this part of the conversation around how to remember that? How do you recognize when that moment might be something that requires you to "board the bus"?

BOBBY: Scott, I think what I've learned in my journey specifically through that experience is that you never know the power of that moment. What it really helped bring to light for me was a self-assessment that I've used to guide my journey. It's a real simple question that I ask myself: Who did I help feel seen today?

· · ·

THE TRANSFORMATIONAL INSIGHT

Each of us holds the potential to be a Transition Figure in someone else's life by knowing when to "board the bus."

THE QUESTION

Who will you help feel seen today?

MARIE FORLEO

FRANKLINCOVEY
ONLEADERSHIP
WITH SCOTT MILLER

EPISODE 95

MARIE FORLEO
EVERYTHING IS FIGUREOUTABLE

I WAS FORTUNATE to have spent much of my first fifteen years at the FranklinCovey Company in the presence of Dr. Stephen R. Covey, the cofounder and author of the incomparable book, *The 7 Habits of Highly Effective People*. I think Dr. Covey may become one of the most quoted humans of our generation. Not just pithy throwaways, but profound gifts of wisdom by one of humanity's greatest minds. A sampling of his quotable thoughts includes:

> "You can't talk your way out of a problem you behaved yourself into."
> "With people, fast is slow and slow is fast."
> "We tend to listen with the intent to respond, not with the intent to understand."
> "To know, but not to do, is not to know."
> "Be a light, not a judge. Be a model, not a critic."
> "Setbacks are inevitable. Misery is a choice."

"As long as you think the problem is out there, that very thought is the problem."

One quote that has especially motivated me from my very first days in the firm is Stephen's advice to "Use Your R&I," meaning your "Resourcefulness and Initiative." I've made this concept the centerpiece of my professional brand. Basically, it means we can accomplish anything when we marshal the full force of our creativity. And this is where Marie Forleo picks up the ball and runs it to the end zone. Her remarkable book, *Everything Is Figureoutable*, is a #1 *New York Times* bestseller, and her success in life is a tribute to its title and value. It's a bold promise, and Marie knows it.

Marie first encountered the term *figureoutable* from her mother as Marie observed her acting as the at-home handyman frequently, fixing everything from tiles to old radios. One day, Marie asked her mom, "How do you know how to do all of these things if you've never done them before and no one ever taught you?"

Her mother replied, "Marie, everything is figureoutable."

Marie soon found herself (and others) turning daunting challenges into figureoutable scenarios. From her own time transforming her career, to helping women overcome patriarchal systems in their home countries, Marie found that simple but powerful viewpoint the key to overcoming hardship and tragedy and ultimately finding success.

My time with Marie discussing *Everything Is Figureoutable* gave voice to a competency that differentiates the average from the extraordinary. That is, the indefatigable perseverance to marshal your energy, focus, and creativity toward accomplishing something that is important to you or someone or something you care about. Marie's transformational insight is that there is differentiating value in continuing to work on a worthy problem and persistently "figure things out" even when others are ready to throw in the towel, give up, or walk away. Note that I said "worthy" because you must know when something is or isn't worth your most precious asset, your time. Her interview validated my own persistence to stay "on task" and emboldened me to believe that my energy, creativity, and ingenuity were assets I could be proud of. No need to continue falling victim to the small-minded naysayers who consistently criticize me for my perseverance, drive, big bold thinking, and persistence in taking on goals others view as unrealistic and even outrageous. Thank you, Marie, for turning what some see as stubbornness and a fatiguing personality trait into a key differentiator for making contributions, solving problems, and providing opportunities, often for others (even when they can't see them).

No doubt you have a story like the one that follows, and I expect that you will see yourself in this one. You might mistake me as the hero of this story, but be careful not to fall into that trap. The real hero is Patricia—be sure to look for why.

Several years ago, while I was serving as the chief marketing officer for FranklinCovey, we launched a suite of highly anticipated leadership development solutions. Pre-COVID, nearly all of our product launches included live, in-person events where it was common for us to road-show our offerings in over 170 cities around the world. We would work painstakingly to market and fill the events with prequalified prospects, train our consultants to facilitate the sessions against a strict centerline, educate our sales teams to position the solutions and products properly, and ensure that all the participants were clear on the value to their organizations and that the call to action was unmistakable.

Among many memorable launches was a series of two live events: one in the morning to overview the multiple solutions, and one as an afternoon lunch to take a deeper dive into the content and answer questions about implementation. A tall order, but we felt up to the challenge.

Fast-forward, and we were a few weeks into the multicity series. I received a text and multiple missed calls from an unknown number, insisting I call back immediately. But since I was sitting in church with my then seven-year-old son preparing for his First Holy Communion sacrament, I felt justified in ignoring all the Pavlovian buzzing in my pocket. But after incessant repeat calls and texts, I finally relented and stepped outside to answer what was clearly some kind of world-ending emergency—or it better be to match my growing ire. I answered and discovered it was Patricia Lambert, one of our Canadian-based consultants, with panic in her voice. She quickly informed me that because of a series of winter storms, she couldn't get from Vancouver to Minneapolis in time for the marketing event the following morning—an event that had three hundred people registered and confirmed to attend.

Not thirty but *three hundred* senior-level leaders, every one having completed a pre-consult with one of our sales colleagues. Patricia, a highly dependable consultant with a multi-decade tenure and a reputation for doing whatever it took to "deliver the goods," had spent hours working every solution she could think of. After briefing me on all her ideas to get to Minneapolis, we pivoted to exploring options, including using standby consultants (none were available), booking alternative flights (hundreds had already been canceled, with more likely to come), and other increasingly ridiculous/desperate solutions (including cross-country Uber). I finally looked at my watch, saw it was closing in on 8:00 p.m., thanked her profusely for her tireless efforts to find any viable alternative, and announced, "Thank you, Patricia. I'll own it."

Realizing flight windows were closing for everyone across the nation, I called our indispensable director of travel, James Thalman, and booked a flight for myself that left Salt Lake City in ninety minutes. I abandoned my son at church (in the care of good friends), rushed home, hurriedly grabbed a suit and razor, and raced to the airport to board a flight that connected through Las Vegas as a red-eye, landing in Minneapolis, Minnesota, literally forty-five minutes before the event's start time the next morning. Although the logistics had been solved in terms of delivering a human to the event, there was a potentially bigger problem: said human was wholly unqualified to teach the sessions.

Truly, directing and producing a movie isn't the same as acting in it. Not just acting in a bit part, but being the lead. You might think as the CMO responsible for the entire campaign, I should have been able to deliver the sessions with no problem.

And you'd be wrong.

I may have been qualified to teach many of our solutions, but this one was new, and I had been wholly invested in behind-the-scenes marketing efforts. But if Marie Forleo was right, everything is figureoutable . . . even this.

So I found some help. I called every possible trained consultant on the drive to the airport and finally reached one. Between the drive, the two flights, the layover in Las Vegas, and the taxi to the hotel, I had him force-feed me the agenda and sequence. He taught me the big concepts and emailed me the slide deck (250 slides), plus the videos I needed to watch, and a PDF of the guidebook I had to become familiar with. All during a red-eye! And if you didn't know, homeboy goes to sleep at 9:30 p.m. every night, without exception.

After my self-imposed crash course, I arrived at the hotel hosting the event, showered (if you could even call it that), suited up, brushed my teeth, shaved, then practically ran into the completely full ballroom three minutes before the program opened. Tucking in my mic, I walked up to the front with characteristic Scott Miller confidence and bravado and announced, "Good morning, Minneapolis. Welcome. Today you are going to have an amazing leadership experience."

It turned out that every single person showed up, plus ten surprise guests who weren't put off by the massive snowstorm. Minnesotans aren't to be underestimated, people.

Miraculously, I made it through the first session (with a modicum of success), and while everyone was grabbing their coffee refill during the first break, I looked ahead at the facilitator guide to teach the second session. Unfortunately, I had spent nearly all my prep time just to make it through the first two hours of the event. I had barely given any thought to the agenda beyond that.

Ten minutes passed (it felt like ten seconds), and soon everyone was back in their seats, and to my surprise, they seemed energized and excited to proceed. So far, so good. I got ready to draw on my personal reservoir of R&I and figure everything out, in real-time, in front of a high-stakes audience. Let me be very clear: I had no idea what was going to come out of my mouth next as I did not know the content of the second session. I was panicked.

Then I caught sight of an angel standing in the back of the room. It was Patricia Lambert! She was leaning against the wall with a big smile. I cannot describe the level of relief that washed over me. I honestly felt like crying. Patricia, despite my releasing her from any further responsibility, had never stopped trying to solve the problem. She had crisscrossed the northwest that night, also via a series of red-eye flights, and somehow made it to Minneapolis. It took an *Everything Is Figureoutable* mindset to get both her and I there that day, as Patricia could have easily just tucked herself into bed the previous evening and said, "It's okay, Scott's got it." But instead, she tapped into her bank of resourcefulness and initiative and kept working the problem until she figured it out.

I called the group back together, put them into an exercise, and effortlessly passed the session baton to Patricia where she crushed it for the rest of the day. Little did I know, Patricia had been in the back of the room for nearly a full hour, gauging my confidence and competence and ultimately choosing not to rescue me by swooping in to save the day. That's just not her style—she is a class act. The day was an enormous success, and the three hundred participants far exceeded our revenue expectations because of our collective efforts. I want to thank all of the Minnesota-based

FranklinCovey associates for their confidence in me and their hard work to make sure the entire event was perfectly planned and executed. It allowed me to marshal all my energy and talents, as shallow as they were, into creating a seamless two-hour opening that set Patricia up for great success for the remainder of the day.

There are many times in my career when I've seen colleagues do whatever it takes to figure out a way through a tough problem:

- An event in Des Moines and the flight from Denver is canceled? No problem! Rent a car and drive ten hours through the night to arrive on time.

- A client's materials didn't arrive for their conference? No problem! A local associate will spend the evening at a local printer copying and binding duplicate materials.

- The catering order isn't properly placed for your regional team meeting and thirty colleagues expect a full breakfast? Hello, Kroger, at 4:00 a.m.

You likely have your own stories showing that with enough tenacity and dedication, *Everything Is Figureoutable.* Could we have canceled on the packed house during a snowstorm? Sure. It would even sound perfectly reasonable: "We're sorry to inform you that our consultant cannot attend tomorrow because of the winter storm. We apologize for the inconvenience, and we will contact you with another date in the hopes it might fit with your schedule." That might be okay if you accept an *Everything Is Excusable* mindset. But holding an *Everything Is Figureoutable* perspective means never having to write that email. And in over three decades, I never have. And I'm certain Marie Forleo hasn't. And for sure, Patricia Lambert hasn't either.

THE TRANSFORMATIONAL INSIGHT

By using your R&I (Resourcefulness & Initiative), nearly *Everything Is Figureoutable.*

THE QUESTION

What are you doing to constantly feed and nourish your creativity, problem-solving skills, and proactive muscles to best set yourself up for figuring stuff out?

SEAN COVEY

FRANKLINCOVEY
ONLEADERSHIP
WITH SCOTT MILLER

EPISODE 103

SEAN COVEY

SELF-WORTH, SELF-ESTEEM, AND SELF-CONFIDENCE

SEAN COVEY IS one of Dr. Stephen R. Covey's nine children. The second-oldest son, after Stephen M. R. Covey, author of *The Speed of Trust*, Sean has written books that have sold over 10 million copies. And in case you didn't know, that's an insane number. His titles include: *The 4 Disciplines of Execution*, *The 6 Most Important Decisions You'll Ever Make*, *The 7 Habits of Happy Kids*, and his runaway bestseller, *The 7 Habits of Highly Effective Teens*.

Now I know what you're thinking—if you were Jack Canfield's son and wrote *Sirloin Soup for the Soul* or Dale Carnegie's daughter who penned *How to Win Friends and Influence in the Wild*, you'd probably have a bestseller, too.

Nope.

The literary field is paved with countless follow-ups that fizzled. Sean's book, *The 7 Habits of Highly Effective Teens*, which is an adaptation geared to adolescents from his father's incomparable tome, *The 7 Habits of Highly Effective People*, had a head start. But the comparison ends there. Twenty-six years ago, when I first joined the company, Sean was completing hundreds of hours of interviews with teens, parents, caregivers, educators, and test readers. He knew he was stepping up to do something targeted at what was historically considered a disengaged market.

I think history will reveal a handful of authors who ignited an entire generation's love of reading (and doing so during an explosion of addictive gaming, social media, and virtual reality temptations). Authors like J. K. Rowling of the *Harry Potter* series; Jeff Kinney, the genius behind the *Diary of a Wimpy Kid* brand; and Stephanie Meyer of the *Twilight* series. On the nonfiction side, Sean authored what is considered one of the most influential leadership series ever written for young readers (and a lot of older readers who found the book's tone more accessible). But the insight I want to highlight comes from somewhere else . . . something that Sean, admittedly, doesn't talk much about—even though it's foundational to his personal paradigm. And in one four-minute conversation nearly two decades ago, it changed how I think about myself to this day.

I had just moved back to our headquarters in Salt Lake City from a six-year assignment in Chicago, and I was complimenting Sean on his book, *The 6 Most Important Decisions You'll Ever Make*. During our conversation, Sean shared his opinion about the differences between self-worth, self-esteem, and self-confidence. They all sound quite similar, and I think most of us lump them into a similar category—I know I certainly did. As I pondered on it further, I remember thinking, *Yeah, there is a difference, I've just used them interchangeably most of my life and never gave them much thought as three separate concepts.*

I've rarely stopped thinking about this distinction since.

Self-worth.

Self-esteem.

Self-confidence.

Which I think makes me the exception unless you're a professional coach or a psychology major. We might refer to our self-esteem taking a hit when something unflattering happens, or our self-confidence suffering as we come off a string of failures, or even grappling with our self-worth because of the increasingly competitive and social media–driven world we live in. But how often do we stack these terms next to each other and really unpack what they mean and how they work together?

Let's start with Sean's definition of self-worth. Simply put, it is the God-given, equal worth every human being has. Now, you can substitute whatever descriptor for God represents your beliefs—Creator, Life Force, etc.—but the point is that our individual worth as human beings is infinite and without exception. Which means no one can diminish our self-worth—not our family, friends, leaders, or anyone else. Not even a swell of negative reactions to a social media post. We are all humans possessing equal self-worth. Period.

Coming to accept that, not just intellectually but in how we think and act, can be enormously powerful. Since I happened to serve on an executive committee at a company whose name carries forward the founder's name, often working alongside extremely competent members of that family who shared the founder's name, I found moments when I felt like my self-worth was at risk. Not in any intentional way, and had I shared this at the time I'm certain those I worked with would have been apologetic, gracious, and empathetic toward my feelings. But it hit me one day that when we gathered for a meeting, there was a good deal of inquiry about so-and-so's dad, or siblings, or other members of the famous lineage. But no one ever asked about *my* dad's health, mentioned my brother in any context whatsoever, or inquired as to how other members of my extended family were doing. I attributed this to me being something less than the others in the room—I was not as important, or interesting, or valued. Of course, nothing could be further from the truth, but what prevented me from sliding into a pool of self-pity was this very idea Sean had shared with me. Why would I assume I was something less when self-worth was God-given and immeasurable? I felt my anxiety fall away knowing I was just as important as everyone else in the room, whether I was asked about my not-so-famous family or not. This may seem like a petty thing, but we all have those moments when we need to be reminded that we are of infinite worth.

Which is exactly the role of a leader, by the way, as penned by Sean's esteemed father Stephen R. Covey: "Leadership is communicating people's worth and potential so clearly that they are inspired to see it in themselves."

Sean recently shared that he watched as his dad lived by this maxim: "I remember seeing my dad go and meet with this billionaire, and the way he treated him was the same way he treated the barber the next day—not that my dad had much hair. He treated everyone with respect, no matter who they were."

Sean continued, "Self-worth has nothing to do with your accomplishments . . . it has everything to do with just the nature of being human."

What then, is self-esteem by comparison?

Sean talks about self-esteem as a kind of emotional bank account, only as your *personal* account: "Just like you can make deposits into somebody's emotional bank account and build trust, you can also do it with yourself. By forgiving yourself, by keeping commitments. By improving and getting better, by finding a natural gift and talent and going after it. And you can also make withdrawals, by not forgiving yourself, breaking commitments, not getting better or not following your conscience."

Self-esteem, then, is how you appreciate and value yourself. It is the mirror that you hold up to your self-worth and decide the veracity of the reflection. Which can be a problem because we're good at distorting our mirrors or allowing others to do so. Even so, we *choose* how we wish to see it. And given our limitless sense of self-worth, it would be fair that anything that distorts or limits that reflection simply isn't true. Which is what happened to me in my executive meetings—I realized my limiting self-esteem was a mirror of my own making and I was free to cast it aside.

Sean had his own experience with self-esteem as the former quarterback for Brigham Young University. As he recounts, "I remember one game we played against Texas A&M. After the game, I was really down because I remembered all the mistakes I made. Next Monday morning, Coach Edwards called me into his office and sat me down. I'm thinking, *Oh no, here it goes. He's going to rip on me. Maybe I'll lose my starting position.*

"But instead, Coach Edwards said, 'Well, the coaches and I spoke, and we think that was the best game a BYU quarterback has played in the last decade.'

"I learned it was easy for me to always focus on what *didn't* go right because I'm a perfectionist. I'm hard on myself and it's something I still have to work on."

The only person who can be hard on our self-esteem, to poke at it, damage it, or distort it, is ourself.

Finally, there's self-confidence, which shifts from how we see and value ourselves to our assurance and belief in our abilities. Which can be tough, because as Sean says, "The world stacks you up . . . it compares you. You're winning or losing; you're first fiddle or third fiddle; you're first-string or second-string. There's competition in the marketplace and everywhere . . . and we are conditioned to think competitively."

Sean believes this mindset leads to either having a superiority complex or an inferiority complex—and neither is healthy. A quick Google or book search will find lots of good advice out there for building self-confidence. But I think nothing builds it faster than simply going out there and *doing*. And in the process, you make it safe to fail, learn, and grow as a result. Which is why I think the interrelationship between self-worth, self-esteem, and self-confidence is so important (and why Sean's fly-by conversation on the topic stuck with me so many years later). Your self-worth is inherent: you can't impact it, you can't raise it, you can't lessen it, you can't bludgeon it, you can't deplete it. And if you come to think and act in ways that make consistent and meaningful deposits in your personal/emotional bank account, you have the resilience to go out into the world and bravely do new things and take risks. The very things that take and build self-confidence. The three distinctions Sean made for me so many years ago, between self-worth, self-esteem, and self-confidence, continue to not only empower me personally, but shed light on how they can fuel each other in profound and meaningful ways.

· · ·

THE TRANSFORMATIONAL INSIGHT

The more you understand the subtle but profound differences between your self-worth, self-esteem, and self-confidence, the less anyone else can negatively impact them.

THE QUESTION

Are you assessing your sense of self based on the measures that truly matter—to you? Remember, your self-worth is creator-given; it's your self-esteem and self-confidence you own completely.

TASHA EURICH

FRANKLINCOVEY
ONLEADERSHIP
WITH SCOTT MILLER

EPISODE 131

TASHA EURICH
SELF-AWARENESS

HERE'S SOME ADVICE to start: Stop telling people how self-aware you are. Because—newsflash—you aren't.

After the publication of my first book, *Management Mess to Leadership Success*, I was delivering a keynote address to a large conference and immediately after I finished, a lady literally rushed up to the front of the room where I was signing books and promptly, with no self-awareness, informed me how self-aware she was. She absolutely loved my presentation because she found it so validating of her own leadership success and competencies—one of which she felt was a heightened sense of self-awareness. The irony was clearly lost on her that while she was telling me about how self-aware she was, I was thinking how horrifically *un*self-aware she was.

I wish her well. She was lovely. But also delusional.

But she's not alone. Most of us—okay, brace yourself—all of us are less self-aware than we think and profess that we are. Basically, we're all delusional just like my keynote friend. (I've now cured anyone reading this from ever coming up to me after a keynote. Guess that's both good and bad.)

My friend and colleague, Liz Wiseman, author of the bestselling books *Multipliers* and *Impact Players*, and Master Mentor #19, shares a story that haunts me. She was once asked by an organization to deliver a customized work session on building a culture of Multipliers. This particular division was at a breaking point with its leader and literally begged Liz to work with their team in the hopes the leader might "see the light" and work to improve his leadership style. Liz hesitated as she knew the team and this particular leader from an earlier life. Ultimately she relented, still thinking it would be a waste of everyone's time. At the end of the session, the leader came up to Liz excited about the content and promptly announced to her how much he loved the program— most particularly because he was, in fact, a Multiplier and could really resonate with all of what she'd presented that day.

As my Yiddish-speaking friends would say, *Oy vey!*

Take a quick inventory of all the business colleagues, friends, and family members you know who have ever lost their job—or less delicately put, were fired.

I'm willing to bet that in a large majority of those situations, the circumstances that led to their loss of employment can be connected back to their own self-awareness (or lack thereof).

After a 30-year career dedicated to the "people business," I'm fairly obsessed with helping people become more self-aware about their lack of self-awareness. And when I say people, I mean me.

And you—but mainly me.

Because no matter how many times someone comments to me about how self-aware I am, I know I'm not. (But for the record—I am very self-aware about how many times I've already typed the word *self-aware*.)

Organizational psychologist Dr. Tasha Eurich, author of the valuable book *Insight: The Surprising Truth About How Others See Us, How We See Ourselves, and Why the Answers Matter More Than We Think*, has dedicated her professional life to the topic of self-awareness. Her research finds that about 90 percent of us truly believe we're self-aware (that would be you), when in fact only about 10 to 15 percent of us really are (that would be me).

Kidding.

Tasha defines self-awareness at a high level as "having the will and skill to see yourself clearly." She continues, "Down one more level of detail, self-awareness is essentially made up of two types of self-knowledge. The first is something we call internal self-awareness, which is knowing who we are from the inside out, knowing what we value, what we're passionate about, and what our behavioral patterns are. And equally as important is something called external self-awareness, which means knowing how other people see us. That's self-awareness from the outside in. What we discovered were these two types of self-knowledge were actually completely independent. So, the journey of self-awareness is really about focusing on both."

One exercise to increase your self-awareness is to ask others what it's like to be in a relationship with you. Seriously, I invite you to list the most important people in your life below. And when I say important, I mean those people whom you trust, who have your best interests in mind. The people you know whose intent is always to make you a better person. Some will be family (some will not). Some will be professional colleagues (some will not). Some will be friends, neighbors, committee members, and people you may know from other activities in life. Make a list of four to seven people in life whose opinions you trust and respect and write their names in the lines below.

_____   _____

_____   _____

_____   _____

_____   _____

Now, set some time to say the following to them: (I strongly advise repeating this word for word!)

"At some level, I've always understood how important self-awareness is to my relationships, but I'm in the middle of reading this astoundingly insightful book, *Master Mentors Volume 2*, and the creative genius that is the author, Scott Jeffrey Miller, has challenged me to begin building even greater self-awareness about what it's like to be my [insert role here: spouse, leader, friend, neighbor, etc.]. Could I ask you a few questions and trust that you will tell me the truth? In exchange for giving unvarnished feedback to me, I promise not to dismiss, defend, disregard, or diminish your comments. In fact, I'd like to take some notes and might even ask you some clarifying questions about anything you say. What's that you ask? Oh, the name of the book is *Master Mentors Volume 2*. The author again? Scott Jeffrey Miller. Now—can we get to my damn questions?"

Okay, maybe not word for word, I'll let you decide. Either way, here are questions, inspired by Tasha's expertise, that I recommend you ask:

- What do you like most about me?

- What do you like least about me?

- What makes you want to be around me?

- What makes you not want to be around me?

- What are some of my habits and behaviors that you admire?

- What are some of my habits and behaviors that you don't admire?

- What is my greatest strength?

- What is my greatest weakness?

- What is my biggest blind spot about myself?

- What is my second biggest blind spot about myself?

- What talent or trait do I most underestimate or under-leverage?

- When I have influence over others, what am I doing?

- When I lose influence over others, what am I doing—or not doing?

- Which of my strengths do I overplay (and thus they become weaknesses)?

- What is one thing I could stop doing that would increase others' trust in me?

- What is one thing that if I did more of would increase others' trust in me?

- If you were to tell me one thing about myself that would transform my reputation with others, what would it be?

- Since you have known me, what has changed for the better?

- Since you have known me, what has changed for the worse?

- What is some feedback that you have given me in the past that you feel I've not listened to or disregarded, that you would like to tell me again in the hopes that this time I would listen and own it?

Now, it's highly unlikely you're going to sit someone down (or talk virtually) and ask them all twenty of these questions. Or if you want to excise them from your life, have at it! This list is just meant to give you a start. You might be asking your father-in-law very different questions than your rabbi, employee, HOA treasurer, or business partner. I think it's paramount, however, that if you're vulnerable enough to ask these questions, and the person you're asking them of is courageous enough to answer them honestly, then you have a chance to gain some invaluable, life-changing insight into how you're perceived by others. What Tasha calls *external self-awareness*.

What's that phrase attributed to countless people? "We want others to judge us by our intent, but we judge them by their behavior."

When these conversations do happen, I don't recommend having them with more than four to seven people, as there is such a thing as too much feedback. (If you can't think of four friends, read Dale Carnegie's book, *How to Win Friends and Influence People*). Consider the following tips as you begin to facilitate these high-stakes conversations:

- Don't ambush them. Tell them you'd like to get some broad-ranging feedback from them and then send them in advance the questions you intend to use so they have time to digest them and gather their thoughts.

- Let them know that in the coming days or week, you would like to schedule 30 to 45 minutes to talk, and clarify you're giving them carte blanche in this conversation.

- Prepare *yourself* before you begin. Calibrate your energy. Put yourself in a calm environment with minimal distractions. Condition yourself to have an open mind and remind yourself that what they're about to say is intended to make you a better person. Ask yourself, do I really want to become self-aware, and if so, how do I need to show up in this conversation? How do I want them to remember me at the end of this feedback session?

- Practice a bit of self-reflection about how you typically handle feedback. Are you offended easily? Do you tend to have "thin skin"? Do you easily become emotional, and is that a coping technique that might even be manipulative of the other person? Are you aware of your body language and the message it will send to the other person?

- Are you confident asking these questions about yourself, and then letting the other person ponder them, perhaps even a bit longer than you'd like? Do you feel the need to interject because you're uncomfortable with silence, so you move on to another topic before the other person has had a chance to fully respond?

Take some time to better understand yourself before you enter these conversations, as they could be life-changing with the right frame of mind.

Perhaps most important, when you're in the setting with the other person offering you feedback, resist becoming defensive. Do not interrupt them or try to explain your behavior—simply write down what they're saying. I do think it's fine to ask for clarification if something seems vague or confusing. A great question to ask in this situation is, "Can you remind me of a time when I did/said exactly that? It will help me recall the setting and atmosphere of the situation and perhaps why I did/said that."

I also think it's worth taking it a step further and asking, "When I'm doing/saying that, would you offer me any advice as to why you think I'm acting that way? I know this may be asking a lot, but I'm very interested to know your thoughts as to why I do/say that. Do I seem overwhelmed/insecure/jealous/in-over-my-head/etc.?"

These types of probing questions are absolutely acceptable so that you can gain any additional insight into how you're perceived in different settings, by different people—ideally by all who care about you. This exercise can have a profound impact on your self-awareness, arguably, the key to everyone growing their influence through more effective relationships. I recognize that I dedicated much of this chapter to what Dr. Eurich terms as "external self-awareness." I want to remind you not to lose track of the value of building your own internal self-awareness as well, and I think her book, *Insight*, is an extraordinary resource to help develop that. I strongly encourage you to pick up a copy, as it's the best tool I've ever encountered for building a more mature and comprehensive path toward self-awareness.

. . .

THE TRANSFORMATIONAL INSIGHT

Everyone has blind spots that limit their self-awareness, which can be illuminated and minimized by asking the right questions, with the right state of mind, of the right people.

THE QUESTION

Do you have the courage to ask others and even yourself to shine a light on your blind spots?

COLIN COWIE

FRANKLINCOVEY
ONLEADERSHIP
WITH SCOTT MILLER

EPISODE 173

COLIN COWIE
THE GOLD STANDARD

WHEN YOU ARE a member of a Middle Eastern royal family and the wedding budget is $50 million, you call Colin Cowie. When you're a famous actor, talk show host, or celebrity and you're celebrating your fiftieth birthday with thirty of your famous friends, you call Colin Cowie. When you're a billionaire entrepreneur and you and your spouse are celebrating your fortieth wedding anniversary and you need to fly in thirty camels to take the guests out to your Bedouin-themed party in the middle of the Gobi Desert, you call Colin Cowie. But, Colin recognizes this is the 1 percent of the 1 percent and you can't build a globally sustainable business on that customer base alone. Which is why he has very savvily trifurcated his business by offering three levels of service, making the Colin Cowie brand accessible to people of all lifestyles, including you and me.

Colin Cowie is the world's standard-bearer for luxury lifestyle and entertainment services. Whether you've bought his coffee table books, purchased his products on QVC, seen him on *The*

Oprah Winfrey Show, or visited one of the hotels where he's been hired to curate their guest experience, it's likely his involvement has left on you an indelible and treasured memory.

He is the Gold Standard, which is also the name of his recent bestselling book.

In a world of unfathomable excess, wealth, and over-the-top indulgences, Colin now recognizes that the new luxury is simply service. Something we often experience in widely varying degrees including those of us *not* riding temporarily transplanted camels in Mongolia.

After eight years of working in bakeries and restaurants during high school and college, my first real corporate job was working for the Disney Development Company on the team that built the famed city of Celebration, Florida. It was an amazing start to my career, and among the many lessons I learned from my four years there was world-class customer service. The term *world-class* is bandied around too haphazardly, but I think Disney sets the standard for most organizations. Whether it's strategic planning, building processes and systems, or masterful execution of what was once simply a vision of a guy named Walt, it's a model organization in world-class customer service.

One indelible impression created for me during my tenure was how we as cast members treated our guests. Now to clarify, I didn't work in or even adjacent to the theme parks. I was offsite in an Orlando corporate office park working in a Disney-owned real estate development company that built hotels, theme parks, cruise ships, and office buildings. But regardless of our title or our prescribed "uniform," we all followed the "Disney Way," which set strict standards for our behavior, dress code, and personal grooming (hair length, how many—if any—earrings, and most importantly, how you interacted with and behaved in front of the "Guests"). I suspect the protocol has been greatly modernized in the ensuing three decades since my stint, but some of my proudest early-career moments were when we would entertain architects, builders, and famed designers in the parks for dinner and fireworks after intensely long business meetings.

When we were in the parks escorting our Guests, we all were Cast Members. I recall being trained that if you're wearing a Disney nametag, you are responsible for the path within your sight. Which meant that when we walked through EPCOT—my leader loved the France Pavilion—we picked up every cigarette butt we came across from where we entered the park to the restaurant's front doors. Which, let me tell you, was too frequent for my personal taste. To my knowledge, as of May 2019, all the parks are smoke-free. But back in 1993, apparently, it was a smoker's paradise.

The point is, as a Cast Member, whether you were hourly and your job was literally to pick up trash, or you were a vice president driving a company-issued Cadillac, you had the same job once the nametag was on—a focus on the Guest first.

The Guest-first focus reminds me of a customer service philosophy well established in the hospitality industry and recently referred to as "end-to-end ownership" by luxury hotel leader David Arraya. David, who has worked with some of the finest brands including The Four Seasons, Auberge Resorts, and Six Senses Hotels, Resorts & Spas, has said, "When a guest has an issue, any issue, whether it be wishing they had a dinner reservation that evening, to a problem connecting to their Wi-Fi, or something as simple as needing more towels, when any team member learns of it, they own it—completely through to resolution. Not that it interrupts delivering on their current responsibilities, but follow up with the guest, closing the loop to ensure the proper associate or department who has ultimate responsibility for it has in fact resolved it to the guest's satisfaction and delight. End-to-end-ownership ensures the guest always has their need met and ideally, exceeded."

We've all had one of two polarized customer service experiences like this in our local supermarket. "Pardon me, where would I find fresh salsa?" And you get one of two answers/experiences:

A) "Aisle seven, midway down to your left."

B) "I'm happy to walk you there myself—there are several to choose from. Did you also need fresh guacamole and chips to accompany it?"

Pre-pandemic, I frequently shopped at Lowe's. When I entered the store, I was always greeted and asked if they could help me find something in particular. I would invariably answer yes, and I swear, without fail, when the associate would "chat me up" along that forty-five second walk, they would uncover three or four more items I wanted or didn't know I needed, and I always left spending $30 to $40 more each time. Not to mention, I kept coming back because I felt like they earned my business and really wanted me to properly complete my projects. They weren't in business just to sell me stuff—they were in business to help me solve my problems or create solutions to make my life better. Perhaps that sounds altruistic, but sometimes ignorance is bliss, people!

Service seems like a lofty ambition now in a world driven mostly by volume and margins (thanks, Amazon). My wife, Stephanie, is a very savvy buyer and now shops almost exclusively on Amazon. She's also responsible for the Millerland household budget so she is focused on price, given our preteen sons are basically human cash vacuums. Appreciating her focus on price, I remind her frequently (too frequently, she reminds me back) that if all she values is price and selection there won't be a single store left to physically shop in because their value proposition can no longer be price or selection as it must now be service. Amazon.com has introduced a level of disintermediation never before seen in commerce. There is no need for anything or anyone in the middle. Someone creates it, Amazon sells it, you and I buy it. It's the simplest transaction in history. Hundreds of millions of customers all getting what they need at one store.

In today's market, to own a small physical boutique or store—or even a midsized chain—you must differentiate on service because you can't compete on much else. And it better be world-class service or Stephanie won't bother getting in her car and coming to you. Be warned, entrepreneurs, you don't have a right to exist. You must earn and re-earn it with every interaction. In person and virtual.

Reenter Colin Cowie, who knows the value of service better than anyone. He shared a striking example of The Gold Standard in our *On Leadership* interview:

Fifteen years ago, I could handpick which projects I wanted to take, and which projects I didn't want to take and, as you know, the world has changed completely.

In the event world, there is no barrier to entry. Anybody can come in. We find inexperienced people take beautiful pictures, they pop up a website, and they're now your competition. So, all of a sudden, all these spaces have become tremendously crowded, where there's more service than there is actual business. There are more services available, and it's completely overpopulated and as a result of that—and we all know it's a very slippery slope—people start cutting and slashing prices and you're never going to get them back again.

This space has become so competitive that, where I used to close 90 percent of the deals that came to me, all of a sudden, I was closing 70 percent of the deals because people were undercutting and providing a lot of services for free, just to be able to be out there. So, I had to sharpen my pencil and I had to be at the top of my game.

We used to return phone calls and web messages on a Monday. Now we have a policy in the company that if we receive anything over the weekend, an alert goes off and that call is returned within thirty minutes. Why? Because we know that the first person that makes a connection with that customer has got a foot in the door. They've got an 80 percent chance of closing their deal because they're the first person there. And we know today that every client and every customer is speaking to four or five people at a time. They don't pick up the phone to call one person, and they'll leverage the one company going to the other company. So, I make sure that we are the first person to be able to make that connection.

Then we do our homework about them. We learn as much as we can about them. We invite them into the office as quickly as we can. And then it's a production, Scott. I make sure that we have an intern downstairs on the sidewalk who can visually identify the client when they get out of the car. They greet them by their name. They bring them into the elevator, bring them upstairs into our conference room. They're seated in one of two seats, which looks through a glass window into the rest of the offices so they can look around and think, "This looks like I'm in a really professional establishment." They look on the screen, they'll see their names printed. If it's a big high-end wedding that I'm bidding for, I'll have macaroons on the table with their initials on. I'll have white wine, red wine, and do all those for those social appointments at five, six o'clock in the evening. I'll have snacks available. Come in, do the introduction, and it's showtime.

I think everyone today has learned to sharpen their pencil and to up the game as much as they possibly can so that they get to create the emotional connection with that client, and they get that foot in the door. So, I think now, harder than ever, we work not only to gain that client, but then, on the client retention side, we never forget a birthday. Like during the pandemic, I commissioned for certain clients jigsaw puzzles of some of their favorite events and had them hand-delivered. I took music from their favorite parties and created playlists. All these amazing things to make sure that we always stay in front of the client and we're always on their radar. And even if they're not about to do something, they'll speak about me and mention me to somebody else.

What I like most about what Colin just shared is that you might think that for the world's most famous lifestyle expert, he'd be able to rest on his laurels and just expect that clients would flow in automatically. But nothing could be further from the truth. Colin constantly reengages with his clients and provides world-class experiences to keep his company top-of-mind for all of their entertaining needs. He re-earns their business every day, including during the pandemic, when there was no business to even earn.

In the opening of this chapter, I painted a fairly grandiose (but highly accurate) description of some of Colin's portfolio clients. I shared this not to distance Colin from you and I in terms of his client roster, but rather to prove a couple of points. Everyone is valued in his world, he earns and re-earns every client, and he's arguably at the top of his game and could easily become less appreciative. How many of us fall in love with a locally owned business or restaurant and patronize it frequently because the owner/founder greets us and treats us like their best customer at the opening? Then, inevitably they expand and focus on a new location. Or worse, become complacent and we never see them again and everything starts slipping. They fail to instill the systems and standards of world-class customer service for those owning the experience after them and sadly, now, in place of them. "It just isn't like it was in the beginning," is a too-common refrain from many of us, which leads, inevitably, to shuttered doors.

Conversely, we all know that one business where the owner still shows up every day, greets every customer and shakes their hand and genuinely thanks them for their business.

This is lost.

It's the outlier now, not the standard. Certainly not the Gold Standard. How many of your customers are saying, "It just isn't like it was in the beginning"? I can assure you none of Colin's customers say that. None of Walt Disney's, either.

. . .

THE TRANSFORMATIONAL INSIGHT

Life's new luxury is service.

THE QUESTION

What actions can you take with your clients/employees/vendors/neighbors/family/friends to create memorable experiences that leave an enduring impression?

TIFFANY ALICHE

FRANKLINCOVEY
ONLEADERSHIP
WITH SCOTT MILLER

EPISODE 162

TIFFANY ALICHE
THERE'S NO SUCH THING AS OVERNIGHT SUCCESS

THERE ARE COUNTLESS insights to be learned from Tiffany Aliche. Money management perhaps least among them, even though she is one of America's most well-known personal finance advisors and authors. Her recent book, *Get Good with Money*, is a *New York Times* bestseller and has over 4,000 reviews on Amazon (that's legit, people . . . my bestselling book just topped three hundred reviews, which I was proud of until typing this).

Tiffany is a former elementary school educator and, like many of us, learned her money lessons the hard way by making mistakes that almost sunk her. But unlike most of us, Tiffany changed her mindset and behaviors and built her knowledge on the topic. Since then, she has dedicated her professional life to educating millions about all things financial.

But to your surprise, I'm sure, that's not the transformational insight I'm sharing here. You can read her books, like I did, to improve your credit score and buy the right levels of insurance coverage. Instead, I want to talk about her brand and, just as importantly, *your* brand and the time it takes to build one.

Tiffany is known as "The Budgetnista," a moniker you can't possibly forget. But her brand wasn't simply inspired by hiring a creative agency and forming a catchy phrase (but trust me, it surely helps). She didn't hire a ghostwriter to pen a book in her name and then burst on the scene with a *New York Times* bestseller as some do with enough money and connections. Tiffany created her brand the old-fashioned way. She built it over nearly twenty years.

Let's take some time to retell her story. And in it I bet you'll see your own.

Tiffany is one of several daughters born into an immigrant Nigerian family in the United States. The values her parents taught in their home are very similar to those taught in mine. Respect for your parents. Owning the outcome of your decisions. Not making the same mistakes twice (admittedly this one took some time for me). Her *On Leadership* interview reinforces the significant level of influence our parents have over us—in her case, for good, but for many others not so much.

When Tiffany pivoted from childhood education to adult financial education, she started developing and distributing a newsletter published every week for nine years. That's nearly five hundred newsletters. How many times have *you* created something five hundred times?

Tiffany is a superb example of how, through deliberate and sustained behavior, one can build an enduring brand—a topic I am very passionate about and which is this chapter's Transformational Insight: There's No Such Thing as Overnight Success.

Overnight fame? Yep, that exists, though it's often ill-gotten and fleeting. But those Master Mentors who have purposely created a brand of influence with others all did it similarly—over time, and with remarkable cadence and commitment. And when they were ready for the spotlight, they didn't stop. They kept creating even when it might have felt safe to coast.

Take Seth Godin for example, Master Mentor #21. Seth (at the time of this writing) has produced more than 8,500 blog posts. That's a blog post every day, never skipping a day, for twenty-three years. People, it doesn't get any bigger than Seth Godin, who is the model for building a brand. He commands $100,000+ for a speech, everything he publishes sells well, and his projects and courses always seem to be ranked #1 in the list of online offerings. And this hasn't happened accidentally. Still, he continues to post a new, error-free, piercingly insightful blog post every day (visit sethgodin.com to subscribe).

Tiffany Aliche set a clear, long-term vision for her brand and then set about making it happen for more than two decades. In full disclosure, I didn't know who Tiffany was a month before I interviewed her. And I know the personal finance space well, as I'm friends with many of its leaders including Dave Ramsey, Jean Chatzky, Chris Hogan, and others.

For those who follow me on social media, you know one of my favorite pastimes is lingering in bookstores with my three sons. It's a weekly (sometimes twice weekly) event in our family and on one such outing I came across Tiffany's book on the New Releases shelf. The cover is extraordinary and jumped out at me. I wasn't looking for another guest in the personal finance space, but as I browsed through her book, I found her content to be compelling, and her multidecade journey even more so. I quickly added it to my burgeoning stack and booked her on the podcast immediately.

As I read her book, I continued to find her professional journey as valuable as the financial advice she was offering. The more I read, the more I teased out the insights about how she built her brand. One step at a time over many years. I truly think it's transformational to understand how brands are built. Tiffany's brand journey is absolutely replicable—if you also put in years of consistent, high-quality contribution and keep your eye on the prize (whatever your prize is). Tiffany's newsletters and blog posts grew a loyal following over many years and built not only a reliable database from which she could launch her book and broader brand, but also energized her social presence, which no doubt fed her courses and other offerings.

A key to her success is most notably the groundwork Tiffany laid. This cannot be circumvented. Every great brand follows the same formula. You could be so lucky as to have a moniker like The Budgetnista, but without all the thousands of hours invested in researching, interviewing, blogging, and posting, then it's just a name with no weight behind it. A model of hard work, plodding along for weeks, months, and years, for nearly a decade plus to painstakingly build a brand that others would recognize and trust.

If you're considering launching a book, offering a course, opening a store, creating a site, or building anything, be mindful there are no shortcuts. In my teens and twenties, I was the king of shortcuts. Everything seemed to take too long to me. I was confounded by why it took so long for people to build their careers, make it to the C-Suite, or build enough wealth to finally retire or slow down in their late sixties or seventies. They all seemed to be missing my genius that there must be a quicker way.

Clearly, I was the one missing the genius.

Beyond increasing your financial literacy and aligning new and better behaviors to it, I think an invaluable insight learned from Tiffany Aliche is that all successful brands, both for products and people, have a unifying similarity: none of them happen overnight. It took patient, deliberate, and consistent steps forward (and likely a few steps backward) to ultimately build the trust and loyalty of customers and followers. This is a timeless principle that either you align with or deviate from at your own peril.

So here's a few additional insights to build on Tiffany Aliche's example from a guy (me) who's also growing his brand:

- You have a brand already. Is it the one you want and what, if any, course corrections should you make?

- Identify specific activities, habits, and commitments you should engage in, in a sustained and uninterrupted way, that will build momentum—what Jim Collins, coauthor of the book *Good to Great*, calls a flywheel. The key to building a brand is consistency. Maybe it's a social post every day, year in and year out. Maybe it's a column in a magazine once a month. Maybe it's a podcast you host every Thursday. It could be a Facebook Live every Monday morning. You get the point: it's uninterrupted repetition that becomes second nature to you. And more importantly, is anticipated and expected from those following your brand.

- Don't overcommit. The best brands are built through sustainability—small commitments continued over time.

- Brands aren't built alone. You need a posse to support you and how you build a posse is by supporting others—helping them achieve their goals, their dreams, and providing value to them. Not with the expectation that because you're helping them they will choose to help you. But because that's who you are. You have an abundance mindset that you generally want to support your posse and if they choose to support you then all the better.

- Recognize there will be setbacks. Brands aren't built in a linear fashion. Put away your slide rule because the line isn't going to be a clean, upward trajectory. Ask any mountain climber how many times they had to climb down in order to climb back up. Expect interruptions, detours, and moments of doubt. That's just part of the process as you repack your gear and continue your ascent.

THE TRANSFORMATIONAL INSIGHT

There are shortcuts in life. But there are no shortcuts to real success.

THE QUESTION

What shortcuts have you taken that may be hijacking your intended success?

TURIA PITT

FRANKLINCOVEY
ONLEADERSHIP
WITH SCOTT MILLER

EPISODE 97

TURIA PITT
ASKING FOR AND ACCEPTING HELP

Occasionally I've had the deeply humbling and emotional opportunity to interview a guest on *On Leadership* whose influence and fame came to them uninvited. Turia Pitt faced unimaginable horror and came through the other side a hero. I've decided to share a segment of her interview here and then I will debrief her Transformational Insight after. Turia is Australian and began her career as a mining engineer. By the usual standards her life was normal and her personal and professional ambitions mirrored most.

Then she decided to run.

Not just a casual jog every now and then around the neighborhood, but high-level outdoor endurance runs that can push one's body to the limit. And in her case, her life. Here's an excerpt from our *On Leadership* interview:

TURIA: I liked endurance running (long-distance running), so I decided to sign up to an ultramarathon. An ultramarathon is usually around a hundred kilometers or for you guys in the

United States, that would be around sixty miles. So, I signed up to do an ultramarathon and about a quarter of the way through the race I became trapped in a narrow gorge because of an encroaching fire with six other runners at the time.

I don't know if you know what the Venturi effect is, Scott, but I guess it's kind of like an engineering term—if there's a lot of heat in a small space (which was the gorge that we were trapped in), it has an effect on the fire. So, we were at one edge of the gorge, and we could see the fire at the other edge. The fire got sucked through the gorge at a really, really fast rate, almost too fast for us to do anything about it.

I ended up getting burned really badly, over 65 percent of my body. I looked down at my hands and arms and they were both ablaze—on fire! But it all happened really fast, and after the fire had passed, I guess I got this real shot of adrenaline because I thought, "Oh my God, I've survived! I survived this crazy, wholly out-there experience and I'm still standing."

But I didn't know then that this wouldn't be the hardest point in my entire journey because I ended up waking up a month later in a hospital in Sydney. And that was where the real work of my journey began because I was completely incapacitated. I couldn't talk, I couldn't walk, I couldn't stand, I couldn't bend my elbows. So, I really had to go through this process of not only physical rehabilitation, but also mental rehabilitation as well.

I've always really loved setting goals. I think when you set a really big goal, it always forces you to step outside of yourself. So, in the hospital, I was told I wouldn't run again, and I thought, I'm going to show you. I'm going to do an IRONMAN® one day. And I don't know if you know what an IRONMAN® is, but you've probably heard about them.

SCOTT: Our former CEO and current Chairman Bob Whitman is, I think, a seventeen-year attendee at the Kona IRONMAN® every year.

TURIA: That was the IRONMAN® that I wanted to do. I'm really grateful that I had that goal because that was one of the driving forces to push myself in physical therapy, to push myself in rehab, to get back into running, to start swimming. All of those little, small, incremental steps, which I worked on every single day, brought me up to a stage where I was ready to do my first IRONMAN®, which was one in Australia. Then I got an invite to Kona. And for people who do IRONMAN® or triathlon, they know that Kona is a really, really big deal, and it's also quite challenging.

But I ended up doing Kona in 2016, so I was really proud of myself over those five years because I didn't let what people said to me stop me. I mean, I took their advice on board, and I listened to it, and I weighed it carefully. But I also knew that sometimes you just have to back yourself and believe in yourself. And more than that, you really have to be willing to put in the work, be persistent, and persevere with it as well.

SCOTT: Are you comfortable backing up a little bit and re-creating a little more methodically for our audience the actual fire? Because a compelling part of your book and your story is about the fire and you trying to escape and hide from it. Can you talk about what that was like to the extent you can remember it when it was actually happening?

TURIA: So, like I said, the fire was moving very, very quickly, so it was a split-second decision I made. Do I go back the way I came (but there was really high grass up to about my shoulder), or do I try to go up the side of the gorge? There was less vegetation, so less fuel for the fire, but I also knew that fire travels faster going uphill. I think the rate of a fire doubles for every extra 10 degrees of incline. So, those were my choices. Neither one of them were particularly appealing, and like I said, it was a split-second decision.

I chose to run up the side of the gorge. That was the way that I went, and I did try to hide in a little depression in amongst the gorge and amongst the rocks. But it was just too hot, and I couldn't stay there. Then, the fire eventually caught me, and it burned me.

SCOTT: Your story is so remarkable. I'm not quite sure where to start because your journey is so inspiring, your commitment to rehabilitate yourself, to become an athlete again. I'm emotional listening to you right now. What are the big lessons you've learned about life since the fire and your recovery?

TURIA: The first thing I had to learn was how to accept help, and I don't think many of us are very good at that. I'm sure you've had experiences, Scott, where you're really stressed out and you've got a lot on your plate. And maybe people might offer their help, but you might not take it on or whatever. So, I think learning how to accept help was a really big milestone for me because, at the end of the day, I had to accept help. I had to accept help from people around me because there were things that, at that time, I physically could not do for myself.

This short transcript doesn't do Turia's journey justice, and I highly encourage you to scan the QR code at the end of this chapter and watch the interview for yourself. As you do, absorb her insights and life after her trauma.

I found her insight about accepting help highly relevant for everyone, especially me.

I'm a fairly independent-minded person. Most of my early career was in sales, which was a perfect alignment to my natural personality and go-it-alone mindset. More crudely put, I ate what I killed, and I loved being both in control and fully responsible for my success or failure. I'm told that I have a ferociously competitive personality and I'm just arrogant enough to accept that as a compliment. However, when I moved from sales to sales leadership, I developed an instant appreciation for the dangers and downside of having a solely independent mindset.

I fully appreciate and understand the differences we all face in life moving through the stages of dependence, independence, and toward interdependence—or what Dr. Covey calls the "highest level of maturity." This is the framework for Dr. Covey's Maturity Continuum, the model that organizes *The 7 Habits of Highly Effective People* (there's a reason this book has sold nearly 50 million copies). Of Dr. Covey's many profound quotes, one rings especially true here: "The quickest way to change your paradigm is to change your role." Become a parent. An entrepreneur. A spouse or partner. A formal leader of people.

There's no bigger career change than moving from an independent contributor/producer to a leadership position. Ask any leader if they would prefer their team members to operate independently or collaboratively and we all know the answer. Rewind to fifteen years ago when I was living in Chicago leading the midwestern sales office for FranklinCovey. This was a time of significant growth for our firm and so we were onboarding new sales colleagues at unprecedented rates. I think the national average of a new sales associate "making it" is about one in three. A 66 percent fail rate is expected. My experience showed me that the person who "made it" was most correlated to how well they checked their ego and asked for help. Those willing to humbly ask the top producers how to spend their time wisely, where to find answers inside the firm, who to rely on for administrative support, and what "watchouts" they should be aware of with current and potential clients were the most primed for success. It was the new hires who had something to prove to themselves and/or me and felt they could just "figure it out" on their own who seemed destined to fail.

I made it clear to my team that asking for help was key to their success, whether leaning on colleagues for information, inviting participation in role-plays, or requesting access to proposals so they didn't need to spend prospecting time re-creating what already existed. I would remind all the seasoned colleagues to offer support, which they did in abundance as they knew it was the key to their own success. Still, asking for help took humility and many new hires just couldn't rise to the occasion. I suspect retrospectively most, if not all, would corroborate that a reluctance to ask for help was the death nail in their sales career.

The Transformational Insight here is simple. Maybe so simple that we're tempted to dismiss it too readily:

People can't help you if you don't ask.

People can't help you if they don't know you need help.

Turia Pitt shared that it took an unnatural amount of effort for her to ask for and accept help during her grueling rehabilitation. She came to realize the difficulty of accomplishing her recovery on her own because prior to the accident she was the epitome of acting independently and being self-sufficient.

One of the greatest privileges I've had in my professional career is three decades of having access to, being surrounded by, and even collaborating with some of the greatest minds of our lifetime. Luminaries including U.S. presidents, senators, members of Congress, governors, ambassadors, Pulitzer Prize–winning authors, decorated generals, and other perhaps less famous people whose path, learning, or recovery are all rooted in one singular commonality: none of them achieved their success on their own. All of them readily acknowledge the exact names of the people that likely believed in them more than they even believed in themselves. There's no such concept as "I got here on my own." To the extent such a concept crosses your mind, I'm here to gently challenge you and invite you to use the space below to make a list of some of the names of those who have, in fact, invested in you, poured into you, guided you, mentored you . . . or in short, helped you.

_____   _____

_____   _____

_____   _____

_____   _____

_____   _____

_____   _____

_____   _____

_____   _____

_____   _____

(Keep going, I know there's more ...)

_____   _____

_____   _____

_____   _____

_____   _____

As you may know because I write, post, and speak about it occasionally, I am Catholic and with my wife, Stephanie (who is not), we are choosing to raise our three sons in the Catholic faith. Once, some years ago at Mass, in lieu of the priest giving the

Homily (also known to many as a sermon), our nun-in-residence, Sister Karen, said something I'll never forget: "We're all just walking each other home." I think it's originally attributed to Richard Alpert, later known as Ram Dass, a well-known psychologist and author on spiritual topics. If you're like me, you likely take some comfort in the thought that we're all just walking each other home, whatever "home" may mean to you. Home might be the afterlife; it might mean a fulfilling marriage or some interpersonal relationship; it might mean retirement; or a retooling of a skill or career. Home might even mean delivering on your monthly or quarterly sales quota. Or for some, life congruence or simply peace of mind.

I hope never to relate to Turia's life challenge and need for that level of help. But if and until I do, I will be using her as a daily reminder to both ask for and accept help from anyone in my life.

. . .

THE TRANSFORMATIONAL INSIGHT

People can't help you if you don't ask.

THE QUESTION

Are you confident and humble enough to ask others, including those you may be jealous or envious of, to guide and help you achieve the success you want in life?

BJ FOGG

FRANKLINCOVEY
ONLEADERSHIP
WITH SCOTT MILLER

EPISODE 129

BJ FOGG
TINY HABITS

SINCE *THE 7 Habits of Highly Effective People* was published thirty-two years ago, there have been a series of authors who have added valuably to the conversation around habit formation. Many of them we've interviewed on our podcast, including Charles Duhigg (*The Power of Habit*), Wendy Wood (*Good Habits, Bad Habits*), James Clear (*Atomic Habits*), and BJ Fogg (*Tiny Habits*). Several of these authors will appear in future Master Mentors volumes as there's likely nothing more impactful in our lives than the science behind our habits.

My interview with Dr. BJ Fogg, the founder of Stanford University's Behavioral Design Lab, was so compelling that I had to feature him as a Master Mentor. BJ earned a PhD in communications from Stanford and became singularly obsessed with the linkage between persuasion and behavior change. Namely, what are the keys that motivate our (and others') behaviors and how can we influence them?

First, I highly recommend you watch—not listen—to his interview because as a researcher and educator he's mastered the use of teaching virtually. He employed some impressive and replicable tools during the interview that I think you might find interesting and worthy of integrating into your own online presence. (Remember, the full *On Leadership* podcast interview for every Master Mentor is available both in video and audio formats through the QR codes located at the end of each chapter.)

Second, before I speak to Dr. Fogg's insights around the power of Tiny Habits, I invite you to pivot from reading this chapter for just a few minutes (literally two minutes) and watch a short segment from one of FranklinCovey's award-winning videos that accompany our offerings. This video is more than ten years old, so like a vintage movie, suspend your critical eye on current production standards and focus solely on the content. Of the 200+ videos in our solutions library, this illustration, moderated by Dr. Covey himself, has made an indelible imprint on me.

Please follow my invitation to scan the QR code below:

Now, if you're the insubordinate type and refused my suggestion, I'm annoyed. Not at you—rather, at me. Because clearly, I've not established any credibility with you such that you took and followed my advice to watch this video. Additionally, I'm sad that you are so insolent that you dismissed my wisdom so quickly and cavalierly. Finally, damnit, go watch the friggin' video—it's two minutes long. Trust me, it will make this chapter more valuable.

Okay, welcome back.

I get it . . . the video may not be Oscar-worthy, but I do think the illustration of the ship is so salient that it should have you thinking about your own metaphorical rudder and how over-whelmingly difficult large changes can be to implement in our lives. I happen to be writing this chapter on a day and time much later than I had scheduled and have violated multiple promises to myself to get back into the gym over the past forty-eight hours. Shameful—it's literally six blocks from my home and I haven't gone . . . in a very long time. I could zip-line there it's so close (if I had the forearm strength to support my weight, which I don't, from not having gone to the gym). Yes, I have endless excuses. It's 15°F outside. I have a book/blog/article to finish, I'm worried about viruses, and I should be playing with, reading to, or scream-ing at my three young sons.

You get it. You've been there. Perhaps you're there as frequently as I am. Which is the segue to talk about the power of Tiny Hab-its. BJ Fogg's bestselling book, *Tiny Habits: The Small Changes That Change Everything*, is surprisingly riveting. If you're in any sort of professional role where you would benefit from better un-derstanding how to motivate other people to act in ways that might benefit them and you, then order it today. (I just basically described parenting, marriage, entrepreneurialism, and the rest of what we call life.)

BJ has researched and taught the principles of Tiny Habits so frequently that he has them simplified into a short and profound formula: balance motivation with simplicity.

One of the biggest hurdles in our way when starting new habits is finding the inner drive to make the changes necessary, especially when the changes seem complicated and overwhelming. For BJ, this comes down to timing. Can you harness the moments when your motivation is highest? And can you make the new task as easy as possible to adopt? If so, you can leverage those times in your life to provide the necessary small changes that will result in huge payoffs.

Take The American Red Cross as an example. Back in 2008 after the devastating earthquake in Haiti, the need for money donations skyrocketed. How were they to meet such a high demand with little to no notice? Well, they saw that individual motivation to help rose almost equally to the demand. That took care of the motivation side of the formula. Now for simplicity. Rather than finding people on the street or knocking on doors with instructions on how to donate, or maneuvering through a large website or network, The American Red Cross made one simple change: a text. They sent a quick text outlining the need for donations with a "Donate Now" option to thousands upon thousands of potential donors. All it took was a *click* and *send* to be able to make a charitable donation. The American Red Cross raised $20 million in just one week.

To further expand on BJ's formula, it can be expressed as B = MAP, or Behavior happens when Motivation, Ability, and Prompt converge at the same moment. Called the Fogg Behavioral Model, we can see it in action as we look at the Red Cross text example— people donated when their motivation (desire to help those affected by a disaster) met with the ability to do so (click here to make a small donation) that also met with a prompt (ding, you've got a text). Want to change practically anything, enact tiny habits that leverage the B = MAP model.

So about me and my gym dilemma . . . let's see if I can put this to work:

Behavior = Me getting my butt to the gym.

(+) Motivation. Being healthy, feeling good, living a long life for my family, and having a stranger shout, "Welcome to the gun show!" when I strip off my T-shirt at the pool.

(+) Ability. Getting dressed, climbing into the car, navigating the six blocks to the gym, climbing into the various gym machines and pushing stuff around—all within my current skillset.

(+) Prompt. I'll set my alarm clock for 4:00 a.m., adjacent to a picture of my face photoshopped over a shirtless athlete (wife's choice), next to my neatly folded shoes, socks, gym clothes, and key fob.

There you go: a bunch of tiny habits assembled into one B = MAP formula.

Will it work? Well, it's *way* more likely to work than what I've been doing up till now. Which is the whole point. So, figure out what tiny habits you can assemble and turn them into something big.

. . .

THE TRANSFORMATIONAL INSIGHT

Small microhabits have the potential to create sustainable and consequential impact in our lives. And frankly, they're easier than wholesale commitments we can't keep—even to ourselves.

THE QUESTION

What tiny habits could you adopt now that will pay off big later?

ERICA DHAWAN

FRANKLINCOVEY
ONLEADERSHIP
WITH SCOTT MILLER

EPISODE 180

ERICA DHAWAN
BE INTENTIONAL ABOUT YOUR VIRTUAL PRESENCE

WHEN OUR THIRD son was born nearly eight years ago, we ceased most international travel. It became just too difficult given all the baggage.

With only two sons we took a trip once to Scandinavia and visited Finland, Sweden, Denmark, and Estonia. Four pieces of checked luggage, two car seats, a portable crib, a diaper bag, and a double stroller. Plus, a carry-on and any shopping bags full of souvenirs we tried to bring on the plane unnoticed.

I will never forget the look the Air France agent gave me when we approached the check-in counter in France on our return flight.

Not welcoming to say the least. Then it got worse when she realized she couldn't punish (shame) me through extra charges because they were partners with Delta, and I had Diamond status. Meaning, I could basically check in a mobile home and not pay any fees.

I vowed that day we were done traveling internationally as a family—at least until all three boys could carry their own luggage. So we squashed the travel bug and exchanged it for a country club where we eat, swim, play tennis, and generally make great new friends. Now remember, this is *in lieu* of spending money on big, annual family trips . . . so financially, I might even be ahead. All in all, it's been a great trade-off. Our country club may not be the Amalfi Coast in southern Italy, but when it's above 100°F in Salt Lake City in July, nothing is better than the thirty-minute drive up to Park City to cool off in the pool. Especially with three cranky boys and a cooler of popsicles: "Dad—they're free!"

"Nope. Definitely not free, son . . ."

I mention the country club because recently I was invited with other members to a Zoom call with the general manager and the finance chairman to discuss the club's overall financial health. The call was fascinating. Not because of the content (no bombs dropped and management is very competent) but it was like participating in a United Nations meeting—everyone spoke a different language. Not literally but metaphorically.

Some on the call were "Wall Street guys" (that's the exact term one used to describe himself), others were real estate developers, some former military officers, others entrepreneurs, etc. It was obvious that everyone had experienced some degree of professional success, but it was captivating to see how everyone "chose to show up" on the videoconference. And by that I mean the questions they asked, their level of engagement (or lack thereof), who was lit perfectly with additional lights (and who was so far in the shadows they looked like they were calling in from a witness protection safehouse), who was muted, who used virtual backgrounds, or who decided to call in from the bathroom (seriously, someone was in their bathroom part of the time).

Erica Dhawan would have been both validated and horrified. Stay tuned for more on Erica and the Transformational Insight I've chosen: Be Intentional About Your Digital Presence.

Video calls are now the new normal for most of us. We live much of our professional lives virtually and mostly on camera. And I suspect we do so with organizational norms that at least prescribe standards for digital engagement. (No, Howard, you can't attend our virtual team meeting in your bathrobe.)

Three years ago, my country club membership meeting would have been a live, in-person event. But communicating remotely via today's technology has given us more choices for how we show up. In the case of our member meeting, twelve members joined the after-hours Zoom call. Two were off-camera the entire time. Three came on and off as their home situation warranted. Two never said a word. One joined while on his boat. Two were in their cars (and were never on camera). Two or three of the attendees tended to monopolize the questions, but only compared to the two, perhaps having recently taken a vow of silence, who remained mute. Or perhaps they didn't know how to take their phones off mute, it's hard to tell.

Now to be clear, there isn't anything necessarily wrong with any of the above descriptions. It's our new normal. However, it *is* a recipe that, at a minimum, can breed confusion and misunderstandings, and maximally, destroy trust and even irreparably injure someone's reputation. Yes, there was some drama, likely to do with someone trying to make a point, work the mute button on the phone, and navigate driving along the road all at the same time. Perhaps I could pitch a new series to Bravo, *The Real Country Club Members of Park City, Utah.*

Or not. Admittedly, none of it was interesting enough for reality TV. But there were moments of palatable tension, conversations that went sideways, and a jab at "getting interrupted."

Enter Erica Dhawan, author of the bestselling book, *Digital Body Language: How to Build Trust and Connection, No Matter the Distance.* You might think Erica burst on the scene with genius timing for her book during COVID, and that would be accurate if you dismissed her previous book, *Get Big Things Done,* and her

MPA from Harvard, MBA from MIT, and undergraduate degree from the Wharton School. She's also been contributing to *Fast Company* as well as *Harvard Business Review*, and is arguably the world's most prominent and credible voice on digital engagement and connection.

Fair to say, Erica is the modern-day E. F. Hutton for all things virtual. For those born after 1980, pause and Google E. F. Hutton.

Not only is Erica academically unchallengeable, but she's also refreshingly practical. If your virtual house isn't yet in order, you're forgiven because at the time of this book's release, you've only had two dozen or so months to organize it. You must not have Amazon Prime—which would make sense given you may be a digital troglodyte.

Thankfully redemption is here in the form of Master Mentor #40, Erica Dhawan. Here's a practical and easily implementable punch list for how to get digitally relevant quickly:

- **Drop the fake background.** Loved the SoHo loft, English library, Cape Cod view, and for a rare few, the Death Star. It was novel for a month. That month passed. Twenty-three months ago. Get your background in order . . . your own, authentic, real background. I get it—you live alone in a studio and there's an alley cat hissing at you through the window—or perhaps a rat. Or you're newly single with no furniture and too in debt with student loans to do anything about it. One word: Ikea. Go get a $50 print of the Eiffel Tower. Hang it. You're done. Grab a $9 gallon of paint and have at it. Today. Enough with the fake backgrounds—when you move, all your edges get blurry and I'm worried I'm having a stroke. So like the onset of COVID-19, virtual backgrounds are so 2020!

- **Buy a ring light.** There's no excuse for poor lighting anymore. Erica recommends the Elgato brand (www.elgato.com).

- **Stop stacking your laptop on books and empty Amazon boxes.** Yes, we see the whole thing shaking when you accidentally bump the table or it starts to slowly tilt to the left. Buy yourself an adjustable stand for your laptop and position your camera so it's at eye level where both your hand gestures and your facial expressions are clearly visible.

- **Use a quality microphone and camera.** I like my microphone from FIFINE. And no, the webcam installed on your laptop ain't enough. You need a 4K, high-definition, clip-on camera to bring your stunning features to life. Erica recommends the Logitech BRIO or the PlexiCam (www.plexicam.com), which sits in the middle of your monitor and allows you to make direct eye contact with the participants on your screen. Increasingly, we're seeing cameras that focus on your face and blur your background. Bonus—that means you can buy a cheaper print at Ikea because you're going to invest in a better camera that blurs it anyway.

- **Bad hair days. No such thing, people.** Why were you able to comb your hair for the past two decades Monday through Friday with no problem, but now suddenly you're always off-camera because you couldn't pull it together in time for the 7:30 a.m. Zoom meeting? Figure it out. If you would have shown up in person to the meeting in your organization's conference room, you also need to be looking good and ready to engage from home.

- **Choose your meeting time and title carefully.** Don't default to the thirty-minute increments suggested by your calendar. According to Erica, the most effective time frame for virtual meetings is twenty or forty-five minutes. And carefully think through the meeting invite itself. The meeting title should communicate the purpose of the meeting, so don't leave it as "Scott's Zoom meeting." The body of the invite should clarify the agenda, set the norms and expectations such as being on camera, and prepare attendees for how they will participate (going into breakout rooms, using chat, etc.). Erica's rule of thumb for handouts is to send materials beforehand for internal meetings and afterward for external meetings.

- **In hybrid meetings, switch up the hosts.** To remove proximity bias, consider letting a remote host lead the first half of the meeting and a live host lead the second half. Erica also suggests assigning someone to take notes, then sum up action items in the final minutes of the meeting.

- **Adjust your rate of speech and tone of voice.** You'll generally want to slow down your rate of speech slightly to help counterbalance the increased distractions people encounter in virtual meetings. However, silences in virtual meetings are even more awkward than in person—you can mitigate that by being explicit about when the group will experience a pause or silence. Erica suggests something like, "I'm going to give everyone two minutes to reflect on these ideas. Share your questions or answers in the chat, then I'll call on three people to kick off our discussion." And an upbeat tone is even more important in virtual interactions. Because 80 percent of your body language goes unseen on camera, your voice has to metaphorically pick up the slack and infuse the meeting with energy. Study the great television personalities, like Oprah, to pinpoint the ideal tone.

- **Logging in is the new handshake.** Erica points out that fumbling to turn on your camera and audio is the virtual equivalent of a limp handshake. So make sure you can smoothly enter a meeting and adjust your settings quickly—if you work often with external clients and organizations, you might need to master this process on multiple platforms. Similarly, make sure you know what will happen to the meeting when you log off, especially if you're the host. Otherwise, you risk angering a lot of people.

- **Mobile or stationary?** If there's been any professional upside to the pandemic, it's been a greater sense of mobility for many. My career affords me the freedom to take calls and even video meetings in the car (ideally parked). But I've likely taken too many liberties here. Carefully consider where and when you dial in and plan your day accordingly.

- **Be deliberate about whether participants should turn on their cameras.** I personally feel strongly that if you're joining a video meeting, you need to be on video. Period. Don't force your leader to address your lack of visual engagement. Get your act together and get on camera. The entire time. However, burgeoning research suggests that being on camera for multiple meetings a day accelerates "Zoom fatigue." So Erica suggests a balanced approach: be thoughtful about whether being on camera will truly enhance the effectiveness of the meeting. For example, if you're conducting a group discussion, ask for participants to turn their cameras on and set their screens to gallery mode. But if you're delivering a forty-five-minute presentation, your participants could turn their videos off without sacrificing much. Remember, there's no rule that you have to pick one mode or the other for the entire meeting, so be creative: you can ask participants to join on camera for five minutes of opening discussion, turn off their cameras while you're in screen-share mode, then rejoin on camera for a brainstorm session or Q&A. Whatever you decide, make your expectations clear in the meeting invite.

Finally—reach out to someone in your organization or network who is ahead of you on this and ask for advice. And oh yeah, read Erica Dhawan's book *Digital Body Language*. It's a superb start.

. . .

THE TRANSFORMATIONAL INSIGHT

Like it or not, your digital presence is your new professional brand.

THE QUESTION

Do you limp handshake your way into Zoom meetings? How many of Erica's punch list items have you mastered?

CHESTER ELTON

FRANKLINCOVEY
ONLEADERSHIP
WITH SCOTT MILLER

EPISODE 153

CHESTER ELTON
ANXIETY IN THE WORKPLACE

I FIRST MET Chester nearly fifteen years ago. We were both speaking to a small but high-profile group of business leaders from over forty countries at a conference in Beijing. Chester was riding the massive wave from his first book, *The Carrot Principle*, coauthored with his friend and business partner, Adrian Gostick. *The Carrot Principle* transformed the global conversation about the role rewards and awards (yes there's a difference) play in recognition and employee engagement. It's a fast, fun, and relevant read that I highly recommend.

Of anyone I've met in life, I've learned the most about branding from Chester. Chester has a clear personal brand—one created with great care and intention—and I suspect if you asked a crowd of people who know him, they would describe him in the same way: He is kind, abundant, and an energy infuser; grateful, uplifting, and positive; credible and well-spoken, and has serious intellectual chops.

Don't let the fuzzy orange carrots he tosses into the crowd during his keynote speeches fool you. Or let the orange shirt, orange socks, orange watch band, orange glasses, or orange tie (fortunately, not all worn at the same time) distract you. He's not just a branding flash-in-the pan, the guy is legit on what he writes and speaks about. But his ability to build a personal brand to tie together his books, speaking, consulting, and training is the best I've ever witnessed.

Yep—lots of orange in Chester's world. Follow him on LinkedIn—you will live a better, more grateful life, I promise.

Fast-forward to his most recent book release (with Adrian, of course) and it's a bit of a departure from the lighter workplace challenges and opportunities they previously addressed. It's titled *Anxiety at Work*. Which goes to show how far we've come—five years ago, *anxiety* was a mostly taboo word, not to be used safely or frequently in professional settings and especially not when talking about yourself. It was a moniker to describe associates, friends, or family members that was prejudicial—and not favorably so. Likely because of the centuries-old stigma associated with mental health issues and our discomfort, inability, or unwillingness to discuss them. At least not without embarrassment or awkwardness grounded in our own ignorance.

Then something in our society shifted. Seismically. Not being a researcher of this topic, I suspect it owes to a confluence of connected and disparate events—#MeToo, Black Lives Matter, cancel culture, the debate about "facts," the legalization and societal acceptance of same-sex marriage, the new freedom felt by millions to express their true selves through the evolving acronym of LGBTQIA+, and the changing landscape of drug use, abuse, and legalization. Then a crushing pandemic, exacerbated by its politicization of vaccines and mask mandates as millions perished and millions more either took their lives, gave up hope, or sadly, disappeared as we all "sheltered in place."

Shelter in place?

This was a phrase we thought consigned to the annals of history—an edict in response to unrelatable events from unrelatable times. But that was not the case, and hundreds of thousands of small and large businesses bankrupted. Home foreclosures surged, followed by an unemployment rate of nearly 15 percent. And while we're at it, throw in the Great Resignation, natural disasters in the form of earthquakes (even Salt Lake City had one at the onset of the pandemic), tsunamis, out-of-control wildfires (no longer confined to forests but in our own neighborhoods), and hurricanes and tornadoes. Where does it end? Or is it just beginning? Biblical references to Revelations seem less and less extreme.

Which is to say, there is *a lot* to feel anxious about.

Reenter Chester Elton and his coauthor Adrian Gostick (with Anthony Gostick, Adrian's son) offering a call to action for us to normalize the conversation about anxiety. Because gone are the days when we all compartmentalized our so-called "three" lives: the public, private, and secret.

Now, I'm not a mental health professional. Clearly. However, I am a spouse, parent, son, brother, neighbor, leader, entrepreneur, and maybe most importantly, a close friend to many. I know Chester's waving of the flag is not only timely, but hair-on-fire, ants-in-your-pants, alarm-sounding timely.

Enter Drew Young.

Reader note: Drew has reviewed every aspect of this chapter and has willingly endorsed my sharing these details, in case you're wondering about my level of disclosure.

Just shy of four years ago, I received a LinkedIn message from a young college student looking for an internship. He was in his early twenties and somehow thought I might be a good mentor, while perhaps earning some college credit and a few dollars along the way. It's increasingly common for people to reach out to me via social platforms so although a bit gutsy, I appreciated his overture and in fact, I needed some administrative support.

We met for lunch at a local café and ten minutes into our meal I was taken not only with his command of the leadership development industry (he was conversant in most of the books in the genre) but also by his own vulnerability. He shared, with great risk, that he suffered with rather debilitating anxiety, clinical depression, and a host of related mental and emotional challenges, which he spoke freely about, and with a surprisingly rational assessment that was normal for him. He elaborated, after some basic trust had been established, that he was both medicated and under the care of a psychiatrist to find a balanced treatment plan that changed with some frequency based on how his body and mind responded.

Yes—all of this in a single interview over lunch.

I hired him on the spot.

I thought if this young man can summon the maturity to share the most intimate details of his compromised mental health, I want him on my team. As you know from reading my other books, blogs, and columns, I strongly believe vulnerability is a leadership competency and, when used authentically and judicially, can engender trust, respect, and loyalty from others.

Soon this part-time internship turned into a highly paid, full-time career, which has exceeded both of our initial expectations. If you've ever worked with me, you know Drew to be the kindest, sweetest, most conscientious person you've met. He's so broadly talented I call him MacGyver—circa 1985, not the current one.

But let's be clear—it's not all cupcakes and rainbows. Drew has dark days. Sometimes dark weeks. He's someone I would have likely declined to interview a decade ago because of my own mindset that someone with mental illness couldn't offer the stamina needed to keep up with my own energy and vision. I was wrong and I want to credit Drew with dispelling that through his insane work ethic and maturity to keep me updated, transparently, when he's facing a tough time in life (which is every few months, not every few days).

I credit Chester Elton for educating me about the pervasiveness of anxiety in our world, including the workplace. Chester, through his recent book, our personal conversations, and podcast interviews, has challenged and transformed my opinions about what mental health looks like and how, as a leader, I can work to leverage Drew's strengths (which are redonkulously vast and valuable). At the same time, I've learned to respect the boundaries Drew needs to set with me to ensure his anxiety is well-managed and not exacerbated by my impulsive demands, lack of focus, bigger and bigger goals, and a long list of other things that can be confirmed by my wife.

Chester has changed the way I work with Drew. I am more patient, reasonable, and self-aware of when I'm crossing Drew's "line" of what could trigger him to walk. As in walk away and work with someone who has greater empathy and respect for his strengths and weaknesses. Now, this next section is in no way intended to fall into what is known as a false equivalency in equating my struggles with Drew's. But I think it's important to share my side of the experience because it may represent many readers' own leadership and business struggles as well. It's not been easy for me as a first-year entrepreneur when the cash flow is literally day-by-day to fund the business and payroll when Drew has needed to take extended time off for mental health repair. It produced a high degree of angst, not morally, but financially. Yes, there were days when I wondered if I could keep doing it. And it's happened more than once. And he's worth it. Every time. This may seem like a no-brainer policy in a Fortune 500 company, but it becomes uber real when your business is you and Drew, and Drew can't work or is at a reduced capacity because of his mental health.

It's not easy—but it's necessary and the right thing to do, increasingly so in an atmosphere where mental health challenges have become as real as physical health challenges. If Drew had broken both arms in a car accident, I certainly wouldn't have considered not paying him during his recovery, or worse, replacing him. But the key to all of this has been transparent communication built on a foundation of trust and mutual respect. It isn't always easy, but as I've learned from Chester and others, there is often a mutually beneficial way forward.

So, in a bold move, I've invited Drew to share some of his own thoughts to two separate audiences: those who experience anxiety, depression, or related mental health challenges (like Drew) and those who lead and work with them (like me).

IF YOU EXPERIENCE ANXIETY

To my friends who suffer with these invisible demons, unseen by the outside world, yet nevertheless felt at the deepest parts of the soul, you are not alone. Recently, I was thinking about my own mental health journey (which I do on an almost daily basis) and came across an old piece of paper on which I wrote down all of the medications I have taken in a matter of seven years. Twelve, to be exact: one benzodiazepine. Two antipsychotics. Two antiseizures. Seven antidepressants. Some worked. Some didn't. Some helped. Others crushed me. My story of anxiety, depression, suicidal ideation, panic attacks, insomnia, heart palpitations, soul-crushing discouragement, and the like began at the age of nineteen after I experienced a traumatic event that left my emotional skeleton fractured. It was the first time in my life that I felt like nobody understood me. I was alone. I was scared. I was lost. I remember lying on the floor of my bedroom at night, weeping. Was I going to make it till morning? Was ending my life the only option to be pain-free? Did I have a future? Was my purpose in life just to suffer endless torment while others simply watched and shouted well-intentioned but diminishing phrases?

"It can't be that bad."

"Everyone has bad days."

"Go out of your way to help someone else and your problems won't seem as intense."

Well-intentioned? Perhaps.

Helpful? No.

Throughout all the moments these past seven years when my main goal has been to survive, I can tell you that it has been worth the fight. Whatever you're going through, you can make it.

To whoever is reading this and experiencing similar circumstances, it's okay to simply survive right now while you try to figure out how to move forward. Remember, mental illness does not equate to mental weakness. The battles you're facing can't even be comprehended by most people. Consult a professional. Go to therapy (which I have done every month for the past seven years, and it's saved my life). Take your medication. Exercise. Eat well. Get plenty of sunlight. Drink lots of water. Fill your mind with encouraging media. Surround yourself with people who uplift you (if you can't think of anyone, reach out to me on LinkedIn or Instagram @mrdrewbyoung—I'd love to help).

It may take weeks, months, or years before you start seeing positive results . . . but please, do not vote against the preciousness of life by ending it. Your purpose is greater than your pain. I acknowledge, recognize, and empathize with your struggles, but take this to heart: your struggles do not define you, but they can refine you. Keep moving forward, step by step, day by day. Patience is key. Things will improve.

I applaud Scott for being vulnerable and open to continuing the conversation on mental health. Watching his mindset and attitude shift the past four years has been incredible and inspiring. Knowing the stigmas that exist in the workplace, I don't blame people for having a preexisting bias toward those who struggle with mental health challenges. For starters, the conversation has just recently become more vocalized in the workplace concerning mental health and the effects it can have on culture, productivity, and results. Anxiety, depression, and other mental health challenges are no longer things to be "swept under the rug" or "sucked up." Too many have tried to carry the load of mental and emotional pain for too long, and it's time for employees and leaders alike to learn a new soft skill in leadership—advocacy for mental health. Now, I recognize that some people are affected so negatively with mental health that they can't even work . . . for the simplicity of this section, I won't be speaking directly to those individuals, though I can empathize. Rather, I want to address those who can and do perform well within organizations, but at the same time experience days or weeks when their mental demons seem to make their professional lives a constant struggle. First off, be open with your leader. Not in a self-pitying way, but in an honest way. Just as if you had a physical handicap that you wanted your boss to be aware of, even more so share your mental and emotional challenges. They are just as legitimate and can create very similar obstacles in the workplace. The more open you are, while still showing you can produce worthwhile results, the better your relationship will be with your leader, and the more helpful you'll be to the organization.

TO THE LEADERS

When someone opens up to you about their mental health challenges—LISTEN. It's not an easy thing to share something so personal and vulnerable, so having someone come to you with their deepest emotional concerns is a very big sign that you're trusted, respected, and (hopefully) able to demonstrate understanding toward them. *DON'T MAKE THEM REGRET IT.* If you refute or minimize their feelings, they'll remember it—and may even go looking for another place of work where their new boss shows more compassion. It doesn't mean you become their therapist—in fact, you shouldn't. It doesn't mean you treat them radically different from others. Rather, it means that you individualize your leadership style to them and their needs.

Do they need more one-on-one interaction?

Would they like you to check in on them more or less often than you've been doing?

Are there professional boundaries that need to be set?

Are you willing to let them take the afternoon off occasionally, to recharge their mental and emotional batteries?

If you're not sure what the answers are, start with this question: "What can I do for you?" (Scott started asking me this question about six months ago and it transformed our professional and personal *relationship). If you've created a safe environment, you'll get an answer. One day it may be a simple: "Nothing, but thanks for asking."*

Another day you may get, "Would you mind not texting me after 5:00 p.m. during the week? Even if you don't expect a response from me, it still makes me feel like I always have to be working."

A different response could be, "Actually, it's been a really hard week for me, and I'd appreciate it if I could take off a couple of hours early on Friday. Would that work?"

Whatever the answer is, listen, show interest, and respond with understanding. Remember, if you don't give your employees time off to maintain mental wellness, they'll definitely be taking more time off in the future to heal mental illness.

I appreciate Drew's vulnerability and willingness to share his experience. And while Drew happens to work for me, perhaps there's a "Drew" that you lead who is fighting a similar kind of battle. If so, Chester and his coauthors have identified eight sources of anxiety in the workplace, ranging from uncertainty about job security; work overload; the fear of speaking up; feeling marginalized, excluded, or undervalued; and more. For the complete list and the eight practices managers can take to address them, I highly recommend you purchase *Anxiety at Work* for yourself. But the key transformational insight for me is clear: no leader can remove all of the challenges that fuel anxiety in the workplace, but they can try to lessen the toll it takes, remove any stigmas attached, and treat their team members with greater empathy and compassion.

It's worth noting that those who experience anxiety do so *outside* of work as well. According to the American Psychiatric Association (2017), "the causes of anxiety disorders are currently unknown but likely involve a combination of factors including genetic, environmental, psychological, and developmental. Anxiety disorders can run in families, suggesting that a combination of genes and environmental stresses can produce the disorders."

Because of its inherent complexity, Chester and his coauthors recommend that a referral to a company employee assistance program (EAP) or licensed counselor can be extremely helpful. I believe Drew would second that recommendation, as do I.

. . .

THE TRANSFORMATIONAL INSIGHT

Anxiety is no longer a taboo topic; it's a daily reality for many that the best leaders lean into.

THE QUESTION

Who can you check in with today to make sure they know you're a safe advocate for their mental health?

JULIAN TREASURE

FRANKLINCOVEY
ONLEADERSHIP
WITH SCOTT MILLER

EPISODE 62

JULIAN TREASURE
LISTEN TO THE LISTENING

THE MOST VALUABLE feedback I've ever received is from Bob Whitman, Master Mentor #13 in *Volume 1*, and FranklinCovey's former CEO and now chairman.

I reported to Bob for nearly ten years and so deserve one of those Edible Arrangements (that's a long time to report to any CEO). But he deserves at least two for leading me that long!

Bob's not an overcommunicator who provides constant feedback. Rather, his style is to hire competent people and model in his own behavior what he'd like to see in theirs. Sometimes you need to tune up your telepathy to know exactly what he wants, but I honed that skill well over the years.

Yet, the most valuable feedback he ever gave to me was without ambiguity. One day, several years ago, he looked at me during a meeting and said respectfully, "Scott, you make too many declarative statements." That was it. No additional context needed. The meeting eventually ended, and life proceeded as usual for everyone except me.

I thought about it intensely in the ensuing days. And unlike most feedback I get, I didn't dispute, deny, or deflect it. Bob was dead on. I did, in fact, make too many declarative statements. If you've met me, you know I have no shortage (some would say an overabundance) of confidence. It's worked well for me over the decades (mostly). But apparently, not always with Bob and so I suspect with others as well.

To remedy this, I started framing my statements more frequently in the form of questions. Instead of saying, "We must deploy this new solution digitally," or "do that and we'll be the laughingstock of the industry," I would say, "What if we considered launching the product via webcast as opposed to live events to be more relevant?" I was saying the same thing but very differently.

This subtle change in my communication style led to a profound difference in my reputation and credibility on the organization's executive team. I also deliberately began to speak less. Not shutting myself down (this is biologically impossible for me) but I did self-monitor more. As a result, my insights and opinions carried more weight and were not as easily dismissed.

Bob and I have had an exceptional professional and personal relationship over the twenty-five years we've worked together in the firm. That doesn't mean we see everything eye to eye, but we understand and respect each other's communication styles.

Did you catch that?

Communication styles.

I've heard most people talk about their personality styles, their leadership styles, and their parenting styles. Rarely if ever does someone bring up their communication style. Which is where communication and listening authority Julian Treasure steps in.

Julian is an international expert on communication skills and styles. His 2014 TED talk titled "How to Speak So People Will Listen" has 50 million views.

That's *fifty million*.

In his TED talk, he talks about . . . well, talking. How do you present yourself when you talk to others? What words do you use? What words do you refrain from using? And how can you be sure you're getting your message across? He also goes over what he calls the "Seven Deadly Sins of Speaking," which is an inspiring exploration of some common ways we speak (for the full effect, you'll have to watch the video yourself).

Aside from his insightful TED talk, Julian's bestselling book *How to Be Heard: Secrets for Powerful Speaking and Listening* is a game changer for anyone interested in expanding their influence. You're halfway there from the work you're doing because of Master Mentor #35 Tasha Eurich. Now build on that with the Transformational Insight shared from Julian Treasure: Listen to the Listening. I've included a short segment from our *On Leadership* interview below.

SCOTT: The book is exceptionally rich with practical advice. One of the insights, as we move to the speaking part of communication (of being heard), was I also was struck by your comments around volume. I tend to be a fast and persuasive, but very loud, speaker. And I don't know if it's because as I've aged my hearing's not as good or it's a subconscious strategy to persuade people, but I tend to talk much louder than I need to. What advice would you give people that tend to talk too soft or tend to talk too loud? How can someone monitor if the volume of their voice is working for them or against them?

JULIAN: There are a lot of ways of doing this. And, again, the key is consciousness, is asking yourself the question many of us don't ever think about: the way we're delivering content. There's this huge assumption many people make, which is everybody listens like I do, so I'm fine talking the way I like to hear people. But that's not true. Everybody's listening is unique, so you're always speaking to a different listening style, and it behooves you, if you really want to get the ball over the net and to deliver your message effectively, to ask: "What's the listening I'm speaking into?" Then, moderate or modulate your delivery style to fit. That's called building rapport. You know, there are books and books on this, which is matching and mirroring people's pace.

If you're talking to someone who's very, very slow, and really calm, then a bombastic and aggressive style of delivery is just going to upset them, and it won't work. So, out of respect for other people, ask that question. It's one of the most important questions I talk to people about in the book. Ask the question: "What's the listening? What's the listening?"

If you're with a bunch of people who speak loud and fast, then speaking loud and fast is going to be brilliant, and you may have to up your game a bit to compete with them. If, on the other hand, you're with a group of people who are very quiet and somnolent and restrained, then it's probably better to tone it down a little bit. So, what I'm saying, Scott, is there's no right answer, there's no "one size fits all" here. What's important is to think carefully about how you're being received and to listen to the listening, and then you'll automatically start to deliver in a more effective way.

Several years ago, I created for FranklinCovey an event for our clients titled "Is Anybody Listening?" A component of this program was an assessment of one's communication styles and determining if they were assets or liabilities. I've included an unscientific list of communication styles for you to peruse and identify each with either a plus sign (indicating it's an asset), a zero (indicating it's neutral or not applicable), or a minus sign (indicating it's a negative). This has been enormously helpful for me to modulate my style according to the listener I'm communicating with. Take your time, review the entire list, and place either a plus sign, zero, or minus sign by each communication style. Then, do some reflection on when might a particular style be perceived as an asset with one person in your life but a liability with someone else. The fact is, our communication styles fluctuate situationally and with different individuals.

I suggest that you look back at your list from Tasha's chapter and consider which of your trusted feedback partners you might reapproach (without fatiguing them) and run your insights past them for further feedback. The purpose of this exercise is to build your self-awareness around how and when your default communication style is working for you and others in your life, and perhaps more importantly, when it is working against you (and most vitally, against them).

COMMUNICATION STYLES

DEFINITIONS

■ **ACERBIC:**
Sharp and forthright; cutting in remarks.

■ **ACCOMMODATING:**
Catering to the needs or concerns of others. Providing feedback based on what others want to hear rather than what they need to hear.

■ **ALOOF:**
Conspicuously uninvolved or unaware of the subject at hand.

■ **APATHETIC:**
Showing or communicating little feeling, interest, or enthusiasm for any given topic.

■ **ATTENTIVE:**
Appropriate listening; paying close attention to another.

■ **BLUNT:**
Abrupt, rude, or brief in manor.

■ **BRIEF:**
Short, concise, and to the point.

■ **CALMING:**
Showing little emotion in an attempt to keep others at peace and ease.

■ **CAUTIOUS:**
Speaking in a way to avoid potential disagreements or confrontation; speaking with precision.

- **CHARISMATIC:**
  Compelling, lively, and prone to evoke emotion.

- **COMBATIVE:**
  Frequently challenging the position of others or the opposing opinion; sparring.

- **CONFIDENT:**
  Certain and assured.

- **CONTEMPLATIVE:**
  Thoughtful, reflective. Involving prolonged thought before making a statement.

- **DECLARATIVE:**
  Boldly expressing personal opinions.

- **DEFENSIVE:**
  Anxious to challenge or avoid criticism from others; frequently attempting to protect personal position.

- **DELIBERATE:**
  Conscious and with intention; statements are fully considered.

- **DIRECT:**
  Speaking with frankness.

- **DIPLOMATIC:**
  Skilled in managing uncomfortable conversations; having ability to show sensitivity to multiple concerns and opinions.

- **DYNAMIC:**
  Engaging, persuasive, and energy-infusing.

- **EMPATHIC:**
  Demonstrating understanding of the feelings and interests of others.

- **FATIGUING:**
  Attempting to get desired outcome by "outtalking" or "outlasting" others involved in the conversation.

- **FEARLESS:**
  Speaking with confidence without regard to opposition or detraction.

- **FLIPPANT:**
  Comments do not address real solutions or concerns of a given subject; not exhibiting serious thought or conversation.

- **GENTLE:**
  Mild, soothing, and moderate.

- **GUARDED:**
  Protective or cautious over personal information or personal standing.

- **ILLUSTRATIVE:**
  Using illustrations to convey concepts and ideas.

- **IMPERSONAL:**
  Unemotional, lacking warmth or affection for others or for the subject at hand.

- **IMPETUOUS:**
  Forceful and rapid. Speaking without thought or care.

- **IMPULSIVE:**
  Speaking without forethought.

- **INDIRECT:**
  Avoiding direct mention or expression of a subject.

- **INTERRUPTING:**
  Stopping the natural flow of conversation to interject.

■ **INFLAMMATORY:**
Intending to arouse anger or strong feelings in others.

■ **INQUISITIVE:**
Curious; asking thoughtful questions.

■ **KNOWLEDGEABLE:**
Informed through experience or research.

■ **LINEAR:**
Sequential expressions of thought.

■ **LOUD:**
Elevated vocal level for impact or dominance.

■ **PASSIONATE:**
Showing or communicating strong feelings or beliefs.

■ **PLANNED:**
Detailed, thought out beforehand; message clearly designed and delivered.

■ **POWERFUL:**
Speaking with control and influence in situations.

■ **PROBING:**
Asking questions from own frame of reference or agenda.

■ **PROVOCATIVE:**
Speaking in a style to arouse emotion or a response.

■ **RECKLESS:**
Irresponsible with blatant disregard to consequence.

■ **RELENTLESS:**
Unending and incessant expression of opinion or thought.

■ **RESERVED:**
Lets others express thoughts or opinions first; refrains from expressing judgment until comfortable.

■ **SPIRITED:**
Bringing energy, determination, and enthusiasm to the conversation.

■ **SUBMISSIVE:**
Ready to conform or give in to the will or authority (real or self-imposed) of others; passive in expressing opinion or desires.

■ **SUPPRESSIVE:**
Discouraging others from sharing or surfacing ideas or information.

■ **TENATIVE:**
Uncertain or hesitant.

■ **THOUGHTLESS:**
Lacking consideration or respect for others.

■ **TRANSPARENT:**
Thoughts and motives are easily perceived by others.

■ **VERBOSE:**
Using more words than necessary; frequent use of adjectives or descriptors.

■ **WANDERING:**
Moving to and from multiple ideas and topics.

. . .

THE TRANSFORMATIONAL INSIGHT

Understanding not only your communication style but its effectiveness with a broad range of listeners is key to exponentiating your credibility and influence.

THE QUESTION

Are you aware of your default communication style and as importantly, are you willing to adapt it to the preferred style of different listeners?

PATTY McCORD

FRANKLINCOVEY
ONLEADERSHIP
WITH SCOTT MILLER

EPISODE 76

PATTY McCORD
WHAT LANGUAGE ARE YOU SPEAKING?

SEVERAL YEARS AGO, my wife and I had a friend over for an evening discussion about some financial planning, as he was credentialed to do so. We knew him and his family well and our trust in him was (and still is) implicit.

Now before I describe the meeting, it's fair to say I'm sufficiently business savvy (after a C-suite career) and have managed our family's investments all my adult life: stuff like insurances, IRAs, 401(k)s, stocks, and when/how we buy and sell homes and land (which Stephanie thinks is way too often). I lead all the details, with her knowledge and input considered on every transaction. Although I focus on our larger investment strategy, Stephanie manages the household budget and all of our day-to-day life expenditures. We may have traditional roles in our marriage, likely modeled by both of our respective parents, but we also believe in a financial balance of power to support important checks and balances crucial to any marriage or partnership.

So when this friend came over, I fully expected to hold my own, but was genuinely interested in learning from him and determining if we should be doing something better with our long-term finances.

After talking him through our portfolio, he launched into a series of ideas that seemed better suited for an oil baron or technology titan than Scott and Stephanie Miller. From the outset he was using terms like *puts* and *calls* on our stocks, using ETFs, hedging against inflationary pressures, and better indexing of our mutual funds and bonds.

For the record, the only bonds I own are of the "glue" variety and sit in a drawer next to scissors, construction paper, and markers. And I'm fairly certain my portfolio isn't large enough to warrant the alphabet soup of strategies he was suggesting.

He left with some gracious noncommitments from us to follow up and then we just sat looking at each other with our eyes glazed over. Nope . . . we ain't changing lanes. At least not with him in the driver's seat.

He was speaking *a* language.

He just wasn't speaking *our* language.

You've no doubt had similar encounters with such professionals. Or you've been on the other side of the conversation as you leaned heavily into your nuanced industry terms, jargon, or acronyms. Should your mechanic announce that your oversquare engine may be contributing to the kickdown and hesitation issues, but not to worry, he's ASE certified and after the LOF he'll fix the pull and play problems . . . chances are you've stopped speaking the same language. Now substitute mortgage broker, real estate agent, nutritionist, physician, contractor, or even your handyman for "mechanic" and we're awash in potential mismatched language. (Professionals seem to forget we *weren't* the person sitting next to them in their licensure class.)

The most effective communicators, like those who've read the chapters featuring Tasha Eurich, Julian Treasure, and David

Sibbet, understand which language they naturally speak and align that with the language they should be speaking.

Enter Master Mentor #43, Patty McCord.

Patty admits to being on the offending side of such communication breakdowns during her first employment conversation with Reed Hastings, the founder of Netflix, as they were discussing her potentially joining the startup back in the early days of mailed DVDs. Read a quick excerpt of that conversation from our *On Leadership* interview below:

SCOTT: I want to take a moment and talk a bit about your journey and partnership with Reed Hastings, the CEO and founder of Netflix, and how you came to be part of that organization.

PATTY: One of the VPs of the company I worked with had left to join a startup and I had sort of coached him through making that decision. I called him at his new company and said, "Hey, you should hire me. I'm kind of bored here. How's your HR person doing? You should do a recommendation for me."

He said "No," reminding me that I'd threatened to break both his legs if he tried to bring anyone else over.

I replied, "Oh, I didn't mean me."

He said, "I'm not going to do it for you," and hung up. If you're old enough, you'll remember that you could press star sixty-nine and it would redial. So, I did that, and Reed Hastings's sister, who was the receptionist at the time, answered the phone.

I said, "Hello, I'd like to speak with Mr. Hastings." (Patty knew the name of the CEO even though they'd never met, and was determined to join the organization.) She put me through and that's how I met Reed.

I went in to interview with him and he asked me what my HR philosophy was.

I started speaking fluent HR-speak. "You know, Reed, I believe it's about integrating the mission and vision to my individual goals and incentives and providing comprehensive policies and procedures that can help people achieve their best selves."

He looked at me and he said, "Did you say anything in that sentence?" Kind of like, "Don't you people even use words? What did that mean?"

So, we got in an argument.

I came home and my husband asked, "How'd it go?"

"Well, I kind of got into a fight with the CEO."

He said, "You know, you have to grow up. You're the breadwinner of this family. You're going to have to be a real HR person someday and you'll be sorry that you keep doing this."

Patty not only got the job but went on to serve a fourteen-year tenure as Netflix's chief talent officer. She also became an influential thought leader and advisor to the industry for having coauthored the famous Netflix Culture Deck, which went viral on the web. It's been updated several times, but Google "Netflix Culture Deck" and you'll get a glimpse into the deliberate values and strategies that helped make this organization unstoppable. Patty then proceeded to author her book, *Powerful: Building a Culture of Freedom and Responsibility*.

As the popularity of Netflix's Culture Deck began to build throughout the world, Patty often consulted with organizations, and a key piece of advice she would offer would be to "Lose the language." She describes words like *engagement* and *empowerment* as nauseating and only distracting from what people should be doing: talking to each other straightforwardly. Or, paraphrasing her book, talking in a way that is connected to reality, allows us to be straight with each other, and act like grown-ups.

In other words, to speak like a human.

Not as a dictionary of acronyms.

Not in ways laden with jargon.

Not full of slang, lingo, or requiring a specialized vernacular.

It's understandable why so many people perpetuate this intimidating style. Too often, many of us in an attempt to impress others with our experience and education, and to cover our imposter syndrome, overcomplicate everything by using a language that isn't understood by others lacking our same knowledge base. I've been there. Bet you have too.

In fact, it's simplicity that drives clarity. The smartest and wisest communicators speak in a way that everyone can understand and make those listening feel smarter around you. Isn't that really our goal? I don't want people to feel less smart around me. Quite the opposite. And I know you don't either.

It isn't just enough to drop your industry jargon, but all of us should be mindful of speaking the language of the business we're truly in. IT people need to speak the language of business. Marketing and creative types need to speak the language of business. Supply chain, operations, and human resource professionals must all speak the language of business, or they'll be out of business. And when I say "business," I mean jobs.

Here's what I think is a great example of Patty's own experience and insight shared through an encounter I had some years ago.

Prior to the *On Leadership* podcast, I hosted a weekly iHeart Radio program in Salt Lake City called *Great Life, Great Career*. Each hour-long episode featured an interview with a different guest, including a variety of authors, business leaders, and celebrities about their personal and professional paths. Occasionally we left the studio and taped remotely onsite at local Utah businesses—typically interviewing the founder, CEO, or another member of the C-suite. Companies like Skullcandy, Domo, Worker's Compensation Fund, Health Equity, and USANA appeared on the program.

One company I recall in detail was Pluralsight, a meteoric tech company that focused on technical skill training. Its chief people officer, Anita Grantham, agreed to be interviewed, so we loaded up the truck and set out for a taping. What was cool was we taped the radio program from their indoor golf simulator (you know, those increasingly standardized employee perks that were all the rage . . . pre-pandemic). Skullcandy had an indoor skateboard ramp and a beer tap that poured freely after 4:00 p.m. Sadly we taped around 11:00 a.m. so I missed that altogether.

At Pluralsight we finished setting up and Anita sat next to me, headphones on, mic'd up, and ready to roll. Ready, I thought, to talk people stuff. You know, human resource talk like culture, people, benefits, engagement, mission/vision/values, and the like. All important stuff, truly. Anita had a stellar career both at Pluralsight and several other prominent firms nationally, building her expertise in what I will call the "people" side of the business, which we all know to be the most vital side of the business. No people, no business.

Given that I'd also dedicated my own multi-decade career to the people side, I was ready to speak her language. I can generally hold my own with any chief people officer, chief human resource officer, chief talent officer, etc. Want to talk 360-degree leadership profiles? Bring it on. Performance conversations and delivering effective feedback? I'm your guy. Identifying and aligning leadership competencies with business outcomes? Let's dance.

Nope.

The band (Anita) took the stage but played an entirely different tune.

Not because she couldn't talk people stuff with me; believe me, she could. Anita, however, answered every question I threw her way with an emphasis on the business.

Their business.

You would have thought she founded the company herself. She knew the origin story, their moneymaking model, their value proposition, and their competitive advantage in the marketplace. She understood their software portfolio and how each solution exactly solved a client's specific business needs. I was really blown away.

Yes, I had some expectations about human resource leaders because after thousands of sales meetings with them over twenty-five years I generally knew what to expect.

This felt like I was interviewing the chief revenue officer; the chief sales officer; and the chief marketing officer—all neatly bundled up in the chief people officer.

Why? Because she'd mastered the language of business. Not just Pluralsight's business alone, but as I've become personal friends with her since our radio interview, I've learned this is a hallmark of Anita's career: understanding the business she's in so intimately that her relevance is palpable to everyone in the organization. She's earned what's called "a seat at the table," something that's been generally elusive on the human resource side of organizations for decades.

Anita speaks multiple languages (likely all in English—not sure about how many foreign languages she speaks). She speaks tech, people, finance, operations, supply chain, product development, innovation, marketing, and pretty much every other part of the business she's in.

The Transformational Insight brought to life by Patty McCord is answering the questions "What language are you speaking?" and "Is it calibrated for the right person and audience?" Are you confident enough, humble enough, and careful enough to speak the language that needs to be spoken in the current setting you're in?

In an executive meeting with the CFO? Drop the marketing speak.

In a meeting with prospective first-time homebuyers? Drop the real estate speak.

In a meeting with a newlywed couple who just discovered they're pregnant? Drop the OB-GYN speak.

In a meeting with an up-and-coming professional looking to make better investment decisions? Drop the put-and-call advisor speak.

Consider making a list of terms you use that may not connect in everyday language of the many audiences you face. Study this list and be more aware of when you should and should not use them as the first step to shifting your behavioral pattern around them. Know your audience, calibrate your vocabulary, care about their self-esteem as much as yours—and watch your influence and relationships explode, in a good way.

. . .

THE TRANSFORMATIONAL INSIGHT

Simple, straightforward, jargon-free communication will always serve you better. But only if your intent is to truly connect with people, expand your influence, and build mutually trustworthy relationships.

THE QUESTION

Are you confident enough in your education and skills not to use them *on* someone else, but rather *for* someone else?

GREG MOORE

FRANKLINCOVEY
ONLEADERSHIP
WITH SCOTT MILLER

EPISODE 107

GREG MOORE
SHARING THE JOURNEY

I ORIGINALLY TITLED this chapter, and Transformational Insight, Your Journey Is Not My Journey. Then I quickly realized that was an old mindset. That the new mindset I have because of my friendship with Greg Moore is that often in life as leaders and friends, I need to share the journey with you—as an advocate, sponsor, champion, mentor, and friend. For reasons I will explain after I introduce Greg, this came to me late in life.

Not too late.

Just late.

Greg is a journalist's journalist with more than forty years of reporting and editing news stories for some of the most respected newspapers in the nation. His career has spanned *The Boston Globe* to *The Denver Post*, serving as the managing editor and editor-in-chief respectively. Greg also served as the co-chair of the prestigious Pulitzer Prize Committee and now counsels executive leaders on their thought leadership as a partner in The Expert Press.

Greg has been my own coach for several years, helping me channel my areas of expertise by converting my thoughts into writing columns, articles, blogs, and books.

He's a master.

Greg and I have little in common other than our values. Greg is in his sixties and as a Black American man, he's had a very different journey than me. I am in my fifties and as a white American man I can't even relate to the bias, discrimination, fear, and even shame that he had to grow up with. Yet we've grown close as friends and colleagues, primarily through my role as his client. As I learned more about Greg's broad fields of experience, I ultimately invited him to join me as a guest on the podcast during the social justice protests and Black Lives Matter movement. I wanted to create a safe but courageously challenging environment for us to talk about what he, and millions of other Black Americans, needed me (and those like me) to know in the aftermath of the police murder of George Floyd and tragically, many before him. And sadly, since.

Greg agreed to appear on the podcast during a rather tense time in our nation and joined Stedman Graham, the famed author, entrepreneur, philanthropist, lifelong partner to Oprah Winfrey, and Master Mentor #18. Together they were superb guests and challenged many of my beliefs formed and even hardened during the protests and riots, one of which occurred literally blocks from my home in Salt Lake City.

I learned an immense amount from Greg as we prepped for his interview, as he shared on air, and even while we debriefed it after. What follows are two valuable concepts that many white people, like me, have heard over the past few years but for whatever reason it took learning from Greg for me to fully understand, internalize, and believe.

The concept of white privilege. Simply stated, Greg helped me understand that the term white privilege doesn't infer that I'm lazy, entitled, or didn't earn my success. This has always confounded me as I wasn't born into extraordinary financial or social privilege. I have worked as hard or often much harder than anyone I know at every stage of my life and have felt, justifiably, that I've earned my success. That I in fact, didn't have white privilege or any privilege for that matter. I've mowed as many lawns as any teenager. I've washed cars, pulled weeds, raked lawns, cleaned garages, and performed every other menial task every widow in my hometown could think up to pay me $2.50 an hour for. All while my other more privileged friends were out water skiing in their new boats, I was washing windows and planting bulbs at Mrs. Gibson's and Mrs. Russell's homes. Not just a few Saturdays, but every Saturday all through junior and senior high. And Sundays after Mass.

Then I mopped floors at a local bakery, washed columns of bakery pans stacked higher than I was, and scraped freezer floors on my knees. I've done it all in life. Okay, not entirely true . . . I have officially never changed a tire and plan to make that my legacy to death. I don't know how and I don't intend to learn, so long as I can dial 1-800-CALL-AAA.

After I shared my lists of jobs and work habits, Greg fully validated me but taught that understanding white privilege didn't take any of that away. And that I would benefit from understanding that as a white man I also had a head start. A massive head start. My parents were educated and well-employed. My mother stayed home to raise two sons and my father never missed a paycheck in thirty-two years. I also never experienced the color of my skin as a negative factor when applying for a job, being considered for a promotion, being included in a committee, asked to run a project, join a club, or in any other aspect of my life. Also, never had I been the only white person in a room, company, or gathering of people.

It was rather sobering when I thought about it.

I had never experienced my race as a liability. Not my gender, either, for that matter. Being a white, educated male was all I knew and saw everything in the world through that lens. Yes, I had a head start. But that didn't mean I didn't run the rest of the race, as hard and well as I could. But a head start nonetheless.

Being pulled over by the police. We talked about the profound fear Greg and members of other nonwhite races feel when they are pulled over by a police officer while driving their car or simply walking down the street. Greg explained to me a whole cultural reality that generations of Black men and women (and perhaps other people of color as well) prepare for and experience on a daily basis when the police lights come on behind them. It feels as if it's literally a life-or-death experience for them every time. Greg shared with me numerous instances when he, family members, or friends had been pulled over for otherwise routine stops and had learned to act in very intentional and precise ways to ensure they survived the encounter, including the exact words to use to make sure they were not killed. It's so prevalent in the Black community it's come to be known as "The Talk," a conversation that Black parents are forced to have with their children. In my family, "The Talk" was about the birds and the bees, further reinforcing my ignorance as a white man about what my friend Greg, as a Black man, has faced and continues to face.

Not *killed* during a traffic stop?

The thought seems completely preposterous to me. Sure, when the lights come on behind me, I dread it and for a few seconds I might even get a bit of a pit in my stomach—not unlike being called to the principal's office in sixth grade. Not on my list of favorite things, but certainly far from feeling like a life-or-death situation is about to happen. Frankly, that's unfathomable to me as a white man in America.

There are many more examples Greg shared, stories obviously fresh in his memory and not embellished for effect. But the two listed above had the most immediate and profound impact on me.

Greg was doing more than educating me. He was inviting me to share his journey, which of course I can never completely do. However, in attempting to do so, it has clearly built a level of empathy and heightened awareness of my own unconscious biases and candidly, prejudices that up until now I have been uncomfortable facing. Which doesn't mean we will have shared the same footprints along the same paths, or that we'll do so moving forward. But we are meant to invite each other into the stories and experiences of our lives. I like how Indian film composer A. R. Rahman puts it: "Each one of us has our own evolution of life, and each one of us goes through different tests which are unique and challenging. But certain things are common. And we do learn things from each other's experience. On a spiritual journey, we all have the same destination."

If that spiritual journey is simply a deeper appreciation of our innate worth, a desire to cast the critical eye inward and not outward, and to bond over what unites us instead of finding new ways to draw divisions, I couldn't agree more.

I have come to better appreciate how, if I'm going to be a part of the solution to building a society where everyone has equal opportunity and our biases are talked about and acknowledged, our journeys need to be shared. The more we understand each other the more in common we'll find and the more our journeys will become one.

. . .

THE TRANSFORMATIONAL INSIGHT

Your singular journey is unique and precious to you, as is the journey of others you may not know. Accept all invitations to share in someone else's journey while also being willing to share your own.

THE QUESTION

Whose journey can you ask to be invited into?

MADELINE LEVINE

FRANKLINCOVEY
ONLEADERSHIP
WITH SCOTT MILLER

EPISODE 137

MADELINE LEVINE
SELF-REGULATION

MASTER MENTOR #45 is Dr. Madeline Levine, a renowned educator, child psychologist, and author of numerous bestselling books including *The Price of Privilege*, *Teach Your Children Well*, and her most recent release, *Ready or Not: Preparing Our Kids to Thrive in an Uncertain and Rapidly Changing World*.

For parents, guardians, and caregivers of young children, I highly recommend *Ready or Not*. Coupled with Julie Morgenstern's *Time to Parent* (Master Mentor #53), you're pretty set, in my opinion. Madeline's insight on parenting and the many pressures our children are facing today (issues I can't possibly relate to given I was raised in the seventies and eighties) is a superb guide to bring some calm and sanity to any home. Not a cure-all, but I've revisited it several times since our interview as the sons are nearly downing me . . . daily.

While Madeline offers sage advice about raising self-sufficient and confident children, that's not what I'm going to feature in this chapter. At least not specifically. Self-regulation is our topic and

Transformational Insight, and of course it's relevant to our children, but as much or even more so to us as adults.

As I reflect on a thirty-year professional career, of all the learnable skills I correlate the highest with those of influence, the top is self-regulation. I define it as the ability to measure your response to any situation, and to summon, often in the moment (at what for me would be an unnatural level), patience, calm, and verbal restraint.

Candidly, it's no fun.

What's satisfying, at least in the moment, is when someone says something I deem stupid to me, about me, or about someone or something I care about, and I respond with the verbal equivalent of a fire extinguisher. Hopefully, you've never needed to use one, but if you've ever tested one you know it's strangely satisfying and messy.

The problem for me comes when my verbal sieges come back to haunt me. The recompense, apologies, and contrition I then need to show the receiving party is always more humiliating than the immediate gratification I might feel in the moment. It's a close tie, I admit, but I also like to stay employed.

No, I am *not* a sociopath (at least never officially diagnosed), so come down off your pedestal and join me among the ranks of the mildly self-aware. Thanks, Tasha.

Truth is, I've learned the lack of self-regulation is just not worth it.

Tempting, perhaps . . . but the gain just ain't worth the pain.

Yes, I generally have lacked the skill of self-regulation in life. I'm fairly impulsive. I interrupt others. I sometimes over-disclose (as evidenced by pretty much every book I've ever written), and I don't exhibit much restraint in my interactions with others. I've improved over the years, some might even say substantially improved. But it continues to be a vast area where plenty more opportunity is waiting.

Of course, self-regulation is more than resisting the urge to blurt out harsh one-liners.

I work with a colleague who recently lamented to me that they were constantly feeling out of touch with what was happening in the organization. Their role has a cross-functional aspect to it, and they should be involved or at least minimally updated on a variety of projects. When I asked why they were feeling disconnected they replied that they weren't being included in a series of meetings that would provide them valuable context to both contribute to and do their job. It's at this point I offered some guidance. I gently but clearly told them the following:

I think the reason you're missing these meetings is because you're not being invited.

I know that in nearly all these situations when your name is raised as to whether you should be included the answer is always yes. But, when it's given a bit more thought and it's asked, 'Will inviting you to the meeting make it easier or harder?' Every time the answer is 'harder.'

So you're not invited. Ever. And thus, you're feeling out of touch and increasingly irrelevant.

Now, the reason you're not being invited is while you make most things better, you also make them harder. When you attend meetings, it's common for you to ask questions, raise issues, or offer solutions that are off topic—sometimes way off topic. 'Great idea, wrong meeting.'

When you attend meetings it's common for you to press a point and then take fifteen of the thirty minutes to talk about a single topic important to you, while remaining oblivious that nobody else in the meeting cares or wants to spend 50 percent of the agenda time on it. Or, when you attend a meeting, you may have a legitimate concern or idea, but in your excitement and passion, it turns into a constellation of sorts—where hardly anyone can connect the dots. And when you do finish, nobody even recalls where you started.

Now here's the kicker. You're supremely talented. Have an insane work ethic. Personally, you're quite endearing and trustworthy. But your inability to stay on topic and not hijack nearly every conversation gets you uninvited. Even when others know they should. It's just harder with you.

If you read *Master Mentors Volume 1*, you recognize my practice of Radical Candor, taught by Kim Scott, Master Mentor #11. Remember, the opposite of Radical Candor is Ruinous Empathy.

My aim in the interaction with this person was to help surface that their lack of self-regulation in meetings, live and virtual, was dramatically lessening their influence and contribution, and candidly, their relevance. Their inability to self-regulate their energy, focus, ideas, and comments was having a measurably detrimental impact—not just to their brand, but to meetings they were indeed invited to.

I've seen this same blind spot exist in many professionals. Perhaps it's their strong body language, profane language, temper, voice level, reaction to bad or wrong news, or a number of other outbursts or distracting behaviors that becomes self-defeating. Often not ill-intended, but always at a cost to everyone present.

The insights you've learned from Tasha Eurich (Master Mentor #35) should absolutely help you self-monitor and get a better sense for when your own self-regulation should be higher. Because it's a key differentiator in those who have the most and least influence in life.

In this chapter, I've provided two examples of adults and the impact a lack of self-regulation has had on their professional reputations (as a reminder, I was one of them). This is also a skill that young adults of all ages need to learn and develop to build and sustain healthy relationships with others—kindergarten through college and beyond. Below are some ideas Dr. Levine shared for how all of us can bring calm and more deliberate behaviors coming off a two-year pandemic without precedence in our lifetimes. Keep in mind, this *On Leadership* interview was conducted in September 2021. Discussions surrounding returning to school for the first time since the pandemic had begun, meaning this was a time when self-regulation (individually and societally) was on everyone's mind, and Dr. Levine had her answers ready to go from years of study and experience:

SCOTT: Regardless of what happens with virtual or live school, what practical advice as a psychologist would you give every parent in the nation, that if our children are working from home for the coming weeks, months, year, how do we balance conflict resolution, the iPad, the games, the phones, the TV, technology? Winter is coming, right? In Utah, we won't be outdoors playing tennis two months from now. A storm is coming. How do we prepare for this?

MADELINE: People keep asking me, "What are the best practices for right now?" The reality is, there are no best practices because we've never had this before, and all the studies on "What do you do in difficult times or during hurricanes or volcanoes?" are time limited. So, I start by saying, "Look, it is an incredibly difficult time, and everybody's having trouble with it. You should expect to have trouble with it."

I have a very simple point of view of how to manage through this, and that is that nothing matters except getting through as a reasonably intact family. I don't care about dusting or sweeping. I actually don't care very much about how much your kid is on their iPad. I do care about the capacity of the family as a whole to maintain some integrity.

How do you do that? What we know about kids and parents is that kids take their cue from you. The list of standard things hasn't changed. Make sure you and your kids eat well. Make sure you and your kids exercise. Make sure you and your kids have some down time. If you have kids who are so inclined, keep them connected to their peer group digitally, just like we're doing. Keep yourself connected to your own support group digitally because we are so isolated, and that is so difficult. And have some fun if you can.

I keep getting questions like, "Well, wake-up time is 9:00 and my teenage daughter won't get up until 9:30." My answer to that is, "Wake-up time is now 9:30. What hill do you want to die on? It's not that half-hour in the morning, so pick the things that are critical, and get some structure in there." And it's different at different ages. For young kids less is more. People are telling young kids things like, "We can't go to grandma because she has COPD and she might die." That's not for a four- or a five- or a six-year-old. They need limited, calm information.

I keep kids away from the media. My original interest in life was in media. A guy named George Gerbner coined the phrase *Mean World Syndrome*: the more media you watch, the worse you think the world is. The world is bad enough right now without making you feel worse.

And meditate and breathe. Do those things help? They do! And they seem so trivial in this time of great distress, but I have several families who always meditate at night together for ten minutes before they go to sleep. They find it helpful.

So, keep your worry level about your kids at a reasonable level. They will do okay.

When it comes to self-regulation, we should strive to keep ourselves at a "reasonable" level as well. It's not easy, especially in the whirlwind of office urgencies or family drama. But even as Madeline shared a litany of self-regulating behaviors to help lead a family through the early days of the pandemic, we too can be mindful of and intentional in how we express ourselves, resist the urge to grab the verbal fire extinguisher, and calmly walk to the outside of the building—even when the fire alarm (whatever it may be) is blaring in our ears.

. . .

THE TRANSFORMATIONAL INSIGHT

Self-regulation, like your competence and character, is a key to your influence in life, both professionally with colleagues and personally with your friends and family.

THE QUESTION

What are your reputational weaknesses and how can you better self-regulate to lessen them?

JON GORDON

FRANKLINCOVEY
ONLEADERSHIP
WITH SCOTT MILLER

EPISODE 73

JON GORDON
TELL THE TRUTH MONDAYS

THERE ARE LIKELY four authors of our generation who have the prowess to use parables to bring to life business and leadership principles in their books. Ken Blanchard, who authored, among dozens of books, *The One Minute Manager*; Spencer Johnson, author of *Who Moved My Cheese*; Patrick Lencioni, whose fame and influence is spread across multiple titles but namely *The Five Dysfunctions of a Team*; and Jon Gordon, our *On Leadership* guest and Master Mentor #46, who has authored thirty-eight books (and counting) but might best be known for his blockbuster hit, *The Energy Bus*.

The parable (or fable) is a tricky but powerful writing technique that most authors swing and miss on. First, business readers typically aren't in the mood for fiction disguised as nonfiction. Why read something that's not real about something that is?

For those few who have mastered this writing form, they've struck gold. I have it on good authority that Spencer's *Who Moved My Cheese* has sold over 40 million copies worldwide across multiple languages and formats. If Spencer earned only $1.50 per copy—that's a nice home on the beach . . . or forty. Not to mention all the speeches, trainings, and derivative products that flowed from "Sniff" and "Scurry." It's a good gig when you catch book lightning in a bottle.

And Jon Gordon has a few bottles on his shelf as well.

Jon's one of the most abundant people I know, and it shows up consistently in how responsive he is to my emails/calls/requests for his knowledge. Jon is quick to jump on a call with our team when we're wrestling with a book project and to talk us through his experience and point of view. And never with anything in it for him. He's what I refer to as an energy infuser and you can't help but feel positive and forward-looking when you're in his presence, in person and virtually.

Jon's books also tend to lean to the positive as illustrated in titles like *The Power of a Positive Team, The Power of Positive Leadership, The No Complaining Rule* . . . I could keep going. In fact, I will:

Training Camp
The Carpenter
The Hard Hat
One Word That Will Change Your Life
You Win in the Locker Room First
The Shark and the Goldfish
The Garden
The Positive Dog
Relationship Grit
The Seed
Stay Positive
Stick Together
Row the Boat
Soup
Energy Addict

The 10-Minute Energy Solution
The Winemaker
The Power of a Positive You

Whew . . . I'm tired from just writing the list—imagine Jon writing all the books!

There's a theme with Jon—positivity. Clearly that's his brand and focus, and it's working insanely well for him (and the millions of his readers and fans, me included).

But.

There's always a but.

Jon may be all about positivity, but he also recognizes the power of owning your mistakes. Which means learning from them and teaching others through them.

In addition to working with many companies, Jon also consults with professional athletic teams. Basketball, hockey, and baseball teams engage his genius to help them build a winning culture and learn from their successes and failures. During our *On Leadership* podcast discussion, Jon shared the following example of an NFL client:

SCOTT: Jon, you consult frequently with professional sports teams, and I wonder if you would re-create the concept of "tell the truth Mondays" and why it's so imperative to building a Straight Talk culture.

JON: For the Seattle Seahawks, Head Coach Pete Carroll has a philosophy and approach that every Monday they gather the team, and they do "tell the truth Mondays." This is where they tell the truth of the mistakes they made. They tell the truth of the constructive feedback that people need to hear. And no one takes it personal, because they all know that they need to have these difficult conversations to get better as a team. So, they have the difficult conversations, they confront the bad habits, they confront the mistakes. They address it so that they can all improve and get better.

We often think about positive teams, that it's about being Pollyanna. It's about staying positive all the time. No! Great positive teams address the issues. They are focused on getting better and they don't take it personal.

I wrote *The Energy Bus* because over the past twelve years of working with teams who have read the book, I learned so much from all the best teams I've worked with, so I wanted to write a book that would help any team become great. These are the principles and the practices of great teams. And I wrote it so that teams could read it together, and if they would read this book together, they would know what it takes to be a great team. They would know the principles.

They would also know what they're lacking. Like, "Oh, man, we have some negativity here. We have to address that. We don't have a shared vision or a greater purpose. We need to address that. We're not connected. And if we're not connected, we're not going to be committed. We have to make sure we address that."

Jon's speaking my language. My first books, *Management Mess to Leadership Success* and *Marketing Mess to Brand Success* were focused (obsessed even) with the leadership and human competency of owning your mistakes, or as I call them, messes. We all have them, everyone knows them (including us if we're self-aware) and so it should be as comfortable talking about them as it is our strengths.

I don't see any incongruency in positivity and truth telling around our mistakes. Positivity shouldn't be worn as blinders, but instead should manifest as an empowering outlook that allows us to focus on getting better without taking it personally. Conversely, the energy it takes to hide, deflect, or obfuscate around our mistakes is exhausting. Constantly trying to minimize or turn attention from the messes we find ourselves in is a total waste of time. Instead, own your messes, talk about them openly and transparently. Then clearly define what the learning is so you don't repeat the same mistake.

I'd suggest positivity flows from confidence. And confidence flows from humility. And humility flows from self-awareness. What does self-awareness flow from? Glad you asked. All the work you did with Master Mentor #35 Tasha Eurich or plan to now because your arrogant self skipped those exercises early on—is about to pay off.

Caught you!

Now go forward and be more confident calling yourself out, in front of others, as an example of what confidence looks like.

When leaders own their messes, they allow and empower others to own theirs as well. This doesn't mean your office or gatherings become nonstop confessionals. All things in moderation, right? But by setting the example that you're comfortable talking about your mistakes and unpacking what you learned and what others can learn sets a cultural imperative that can't be denied. Balance your strengths with an awareness and openness to talk about your weaknesses/mistakes/messes and people will naturally gravitate toward you. You will set the standard for what is and is not talked about, how courageous your team conversations are, and how willing others around you are to surface their own challenges, fears, and setbacks, and how safe it will be to offer plans for improvement.

This is the type of culture everyone wants to work in—where one bold person makes it safe to surface mistakes and everyone breathes a collective sigh of relief. In a recent *On Leadership* interview with Stephen M. R. Covey, I asked him what the best way was for any leader to change the culture of their teams. His answer was shockingly concise and penetrating: "The leader goes first."

Will you be that one person who goes first?

・・・

THE TRANSFORMATIONAL INSIGHT

Great leaders build great cultures that include an equal mix of positivity and accountability.

THE QUESTION

How will you create your version of Tell the Truth Mondays and build them into Tell the Truth Always?

PATRICK BET-DAVID

FRANKLINCOVEY
ONLEADERSHIP
WITH SCOTT MILLER

EPISODE 136

PATRICK BET-DAVID
YOUR FUTURE TRUTH

Talk about a success story—Patrick Bet-David is the model of achieving the American Dream. Persian by birth, Patrick's family fled Iran during the 1970s revolution and spent time in a refugee camp as a small child (which he remembers clearly), before resettling and building a life in California.

He talks freely about his early struggles in life to earn a living, find his place in America, and build the life he wanted for himself and his future family. His insurance business exploded and as his influence rose on social media, he built one of the world's most subscribed-to YouTube channels, Valuetainment. Recently, he authored a book that is one of my top ten favorites, titled *Your Next Five Moves: Master the Art of Business Strategy*. His book uses chess as a metaphor for making your life and business choices.

I like chess and I am a novice player. I understand all the pieces—how they move—and enjoy a game where I typically get my arse kicked. To be honest, I get kicked routinely by my middle son Smith who is ten. (Chess is a required class in their school—which is one of the main reasons we selected it and monthly, miraculously, scrape together the tuition.) Chess teaches superb life skills to those who play, including delayed gratification, looking around corners as to what's next, and perhaps most importantly, it builds a strategic thinking competency. Or to quote Patrick, to think five moves ahead.

I can see this in my son, Smith, as he assesses each piece, their capabilities and limitations, and looks to how different moves might unfold as he selects his strategy. I have won against him exactly once.

I'm fifty-four. He's ten.

Ask me how proud I am when I lose to him after giving it all of my intellectual capacity (I'm rarely able to think more than two moves ahead) while he's humoring me.

So insulting. So emasculating to me. So proud of him!

I highly recommend *Your Next Five Moves*. Patrick's *On Leadership* interview is a must-watch. Certainly, he has charisma and boundless energy, which I find contagious and inspiring, but there are so many lessons to learn from his journey. Patrick demonstrates a litany of traits I am trying to instill in our three young sons: grit, determination, self-respect, forgiveness (of others and of yourself), and vision—what he calls *Your Future Truth*.

The moment I interviewed Patrick, I knew he'd be a featured Mentor in this volume. His Transformational Insight, Your Future Truth, is now something I implement daily into my life through how I think, speak, behave, and live.

Earlier in the book I featured Maria Forleo, Master Mentor #33, and I've never forgotten something she said in our interview. When she has a goal she wants to accomplish, she writes it down a hundred times a day.

Every day.

She writes out the goal, pen to paper, longhand every day, a hundred times a day until it's accomplished. Obviously, Marie is actualizing the wisdom of visualizing your goals to bring them to reality.

The same is true for Patrick but he takes it perhaps a step further. A giant step further.

Your Future Truth is about living your life now as if your future goal has already been accomplished—talking in the present as if your ideal future exists right now.

Now, you might be wondering if living Your Future Truth runs the risk of you becoming a fraud and a liar. The main difference (at least how I see it) is that those who embellish do so to others; those who speak their future truth do so to themselves. Living your life in Your Future Truth is about your self-talk. How you choose to believe in yourself; how you condition your thoughts and mindset to own your future.

Do you believe Your Future Truth is possible?

Do you believe it is real?

This is very different than someone who fabricates some event, person, or themselves that they know is both not true and isn't going to become true. That's called lying.

Living Your Future Truth requires some humility and confidence. Let me shift gears for one second to explain what I mean. Another book I'm a raving fan of is *The Everyday Hero Manifesto* by Robin Sharma. You likely know him from his blockbuster bestseller, *The Monk Who Sold His Ferrari*, which combined with his other books have sold over 20 million copies. That's mind-blowing to me.

Robin opens *The Everyday Hero Manifesto* with a focus on positive self-talk and putting your naysayers in context. I have a self-conferred PhD in compartmentalizing my naysayers (please refer to me in the future as Dr. Miller). To live in Your Future Truth, you need to block out all external and internal negativity.

Let me borrow a few lines from Robin to help make Patrick's Future Truth point:

Stepping into the person you've always imagined you could be is a trained result—available to anyone willing to open themselves up, do the work, and run the practices that make magic real. Life really does favor the obsessed. Great fortune truly does shine on those mesmerized by their gorgeous ambitions. Trust not your detractors. Pay no attention to your diminishers. Ignore your discouragers. They do not know of the wonders within you.

There's no shortage of research and psychology that speaks to the power of positive self-talk and its impact on our beliefs. I'm not a perfect model of this, but after reading Patrick's and Robin's recent books I have completely eliminated any negative self-talk and also that of those around me who I know don't have my success or best interests in mind. And sometimes they do have my best interests in mind but their jealousy and envy of my energy, focus, discipline, and herculean work ethic negatively impacts my mindset.

Simply stated, I don't speak about myself negatively and allow no one else in my presence to either. Have at it in my absence. Candidly, your opinion of me doesn't matter to me, I'm too busy living my Future Truth.

Here's where our sidetrack meets the main road again: I am convinced there is a direct connection between my elimination of all negative self-talk and my ability to live in my Future Truth. Whether it be about a new home I want, a future bestselling book I intend to write, an elusive podcast guest I expect to land, or a large client opportunity I'm sure I will close. My current reality and my Future Truth have blurred, and that's a powerful igniter of my creativity and self-confidence. I don't think my family, close friends, clients, and business partners and advisors would tell you I'm arrogant or full of self-puffery. To the contrary, I think they would tell you I've replaced a former life of self-doubt with a current and future life of confidence and self-love, while realistically knowing my own limitations and pushing past or through those that might hijack me living my Future Truth.

What is the downside to this practice? Perhaps living a life full of delusions. Ideas that will never come to fruition because all you do is talk about them and never do anything about them. As Patrick writes in *Your Next Five Moves*:

> The most dangerous unhappy people I've met are those who are both extremely ambitious and extremely lazy. What this combination produces is envy, which is a deadly sin that will make your life a living hell. These are people who think big and want to do something big, but they're not willing to put in the work to earn it. They'll cheat. They'll throw you under the bus. They're constantly looking for shortcuts. And if someone else has what they want, it eats away at their very soul. If someone is winning at a higher level than you are, either lower your expectations to match your work ethic or increase your work ethic to exceed your expectations. If you do neither, you'll be miserable. What it all boils down to is that alignment is the key to fulfillment.

I once heard a phrase that I may slaughter here, "Many an elevator operator talked often of grand dreams." Forgive me if you've seen or heard it stated differently, but the idea is clear.

Are you that person who announces bold commitments and talks a great game in their personal and professional circles? Always speaking about what you plan to do, intend to do, but when others look back at your track record, it rarely, if ever, matches your previous proclamations? Or are you that person who has a great, bold vision for your life and through positive self-talk, hard work, focus, and unrelenting discipline, goes out and makes it happen?

. . .

THE TRANSFORMATIONAL INSIGHT

Combining the power of how you think, speak, behave, and live is
the catalyst for making your Future Truth your Present Truth.

THE QUESTION

Based on what you're saying and doing today, what will your Future Truth look like?

RITA McGRATH

FRANKLINCOVEY
ONLEADERSHIP
WITH SCOTT MILLER

EPISODE 117

RITA McGRATH
SEEING AROUND CORNERS

A GOOD FRIEND of mine purchased his first vehicle as a high school sophomore in 1983. It was a canary yellow 1969 Camaro—a loud, powerful, and fast muscle car held together with equal parts duct tape and banding wire. The car would backfire, loudly and with regularity, and had a small bar above the passenger glove box named the "Oh [expletive] handle." Given that my friend was a newly minted sixteen-year-old driver behind the wheel of that kind of car, you can imagine the "Oh [expletive] handle" got a lot of use (and he confirms it did). Keep in mind, there wasn't a similar bar on the driver's side of the car, only the passenger's. Oddly enough, you might have the same kind of setup going on in your organization, just swap out the sixteen-year-old driver with the CEO. (Didn't see that one coming, did you?)

I promise I'll return to the analogy in a moment, but first, I want to introduce Master Mentor #48, Rita McGrath.

Not only is Rita McGrath a class act, she's exactly what I think of when I'm differentiating between someone who is smart and someone who is wise. To be clear, not all smart people are wise, but all wise people are smart—at least in my experience.

Rita is a strategy professor at the Columbia Business School, and a strategic advisor to CEOs, boards, and entrepreneurs. She earned a PhD focused on strategy, entrepreneurship, and innovation from The Wharton School (you'll read more on my relationship with the Wharton name in chapter twenty-four), and she's the founder of the consulting firm Valize. She recently published the masterpiece *Seeing Around Corners: How to Spot Inflection Points in Business Before They Happen.*

Like some of the other Master Mentors I've featured in both volumes, I came across Rita's book on one of my weekly outings with the three sons to our local Barnes & Noble. It had just been published and thus had prime placement in the Bestsellers/New Releases shelf and I fell for it instantly. I'd heard of Rita prior to seeing her book—in the CEO world, she's earned the same respect as advisors like Ram Charan, Marshall Goldsmith, and a few rare others.

Rita's authored or coauthored numerous seminal books including *Discovery-Driven Growth, The Entrepreneurial Mindset,* and *The End of Competitive Advantage.* Just as notably, she is featured in HBR's 10 Must Reads on Business Model Innovations as a contributor with the likes of the late Clayton Christensen who before his passing, wrote the gracious foreword for *Seeing Around Corners.*

Rita's *On Leadership* interview followed a similar format that I pivot to when a guest, typically an author, addresses a broad range of topics and I want to "water-ski" across as many insights as possible. I've followed this water-skiing format with Matthew McConaughey, Guy Kawasaki, Elizabeth Smart, Robin Sharma, and several others, and it works, when employed judiciously.

With Rita, it was challenging to pick which topic I wanted to feature as her single Transformational Insight. The title of her book is a leadership competency. The ability, as I would say, to look (see) around corners is something that leaders must learn, typically the hard way, by being burned. Meaning their confidence, arrogance, and omniscience teaches them (us all) hopefully only once, that we can't control or predict the future. But what we can do is learn to see trends, patterns, and recognizable signals, which can prove to be invaluable as we're building and refining our strategies in an exhaustingly shifting marketplace.

You'll need to read (digest) *Seeing Around Corners* to absorb all the actionable bits of wisdom Rita shares from her broad and deep business experience. But I will share one insight that I think is transformational: Rita very effectively uses a car steering wheel as an analogy for how many leaders make (announce) strategy changes and the resulting impact they have across the organization. You don't need to be the CEO of a Fortune 500 to benefit from this Transformational Insight. I've thought about it numerous times when I'm debating (arguing) with my wife, Stephanie, about some Millerland issue. For example, like when I'm wanting to relocate an especially disrespectful son as I research boarding schools in the Northeast, or daily in how I lead my own company and tell members of my team, "Now today we're headed in this direction," when they all know that will likely change tomorrow. Remember the story of my friend and his 1969 Camaro? Let me pay it off now with a partial transcript of my *On Leadership* interview with Rita:

SCOTT: You share another concept around the steering wheel. I'm going to read from the book, if you don't mind, a couple of sentences and then you can expound.

I quote you when you say, "I'm fond of an analogy to driving. When you can see far ahead, you can adjust your trajectory with a small move of the steering wheel; but when you see only after the inflection point is upon you, it requires a big jerk of the steering wheel. Put another way, when you can see an obstacle far down the road, you need to make a very small adjustment with your steering wheel. But when the obstacle is suddenly in front of your car, you have to quickly and drastically turn the wheel in a big, big way."

Talk a bit about the role that leaders play in anticipating seeing inflection points. Are there some things that you've learned in all your consulting opportunities and research and writing that are common mistakes leaders make in not anticipating and seeing inflection points? Are there things you can perhaps remind senior leaders to do?

RITA: I think one of the misconceptions that a lot of the leaders I work with have is that a big change requires a massive response. So, you'll hear, "Double down! All hands on deck! We've got to march forward and see this thing through!" And usually that's a mistake. In the book, I talk about the BBC, which tried to digitize everything all at once, and it was just a big disaster that cost them nearly a hundred million pounds.

Instead, what I think you want to be doing is really using what I call a "discovery-driven approach." I think that's very relevant to any kind of high-uncertainty situation, where you plan as far as you can see, get to that point, look around and say, "Okay, what have we learned about our assumptions? And how can we plan for the next step?"

It's that leadership pressure to continually build up a better understanding of what our assumptions are that I think is so vital to managing in an uncertain environment. It's usually a mistake to do a great, big, bet-the-company, all-hands-on-deck, sudden thing before you've really had a chance to do some learning. So, in a weird way, the way to deal with massive change is incrementally.

Allow me to add a little to Rita's analogy. The massive disruption caused by jerking the wheel feels differently to the passengers in the car than the driver/CEO. The driver/CEO is gripping the wheel tightly, they're anticipating the pull, they have an anchor that will minimize the effect. But for the poor passengers (everyone else in the organization), they'll get tossed around and understand the need for an "Oh [expletive] handle." Which my friend aptly named and anyone having to reach for one will readily concur. Instead of harsh course corrections, the most effective leaders look ahead and make incremental adjustments as they go. Or as Rita would likely say, they focus on *seeing* around corners so they're not having to suddenly jerk the wheel and *swerve* around them. Doing the former makes for a more intentional trip and a smoother ride. Doing the latter will have your organization/passengers reaching for the "Oh [expletive] handle" time and time again until they've had enough and find a different car (and driver) to continue their professional journey with. Certainly there are times when crises or unforeseen events necessitate a quick jerk of the wheel. Be sure that's not your default leadership strategy and only employ it in true times of need. Your passengers only want to hear a "hold on!" on rare occasions.

. . .

THE TRANSFORMATIONAL INSIGHT

Sometimes incremental change ultimately brings faster results. Knowing when to go big and fast or small and slow is often the difference between being smart and being wise.

THE QUESTION

How many "Oh [expletive] handles" have you had to install in your organization's culture to accommodate your sudden jerking of the wheel?

GEOFFREY MOORE

FRANKLINCOVEY
ONLEADERSHIP
WITH SCOTT MILLER

EPISODE 80

GEOFFREY MOORE
CROSSING THE CHASM

WHETHER YOU ARE selling lingerie, tulips, iced tea, software, or medical devices, every company is now a technology company. And every company is in the same business: the people business or, stated differently, the business of relationships. If you accept that premise, you are probably aware or should be aware of the technology adoption life cycle (more formally called the Diffusion of Innovation Theory developed by Everett Rogers), which is a model that illustrates five distinct characteristics of adoption over a bell curve or normal distribution. There are five groups of individuals based on demographic and psychographic profiles: innovators, early adopters, early majority, late majority, and laggards.

This model has been subsequently adapted over the course of the twentieth century, perhaps most profoundly by Master Mentor #49 Geoffrey Moore in his perennial bestselling book *Crossing the Chasm*, which has sold more than a million copies. It is often referred to as a technology bible for any startup in Silicon Valley.

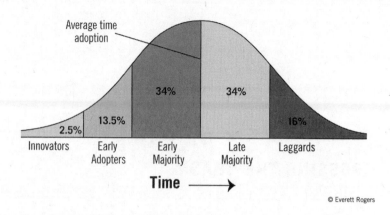

Average time adoption

2.5%	13.5%	34%	34%	16%
Innovators	Early Adopters	Early Majority	Late Majority	Laggards

Time ⟶

© Everett Rogers

Geoffrey's book has also been read by every chief marketing officer, chief sales officer, and chief product innovations officer as they consider how best to roll out their products.

To best communicate how Geoffrey identifies a crucial chasm within this distribution model, I have included a partial transcript of our *On Leadership* interview. As you read this, think less about which one of these you identify with and more about how your business is using this highly valuable research to ensure that your R&D, product testing, soft launch, and public launch strategies are calibrated properly and best maximized.

CROSSING THE CHASM

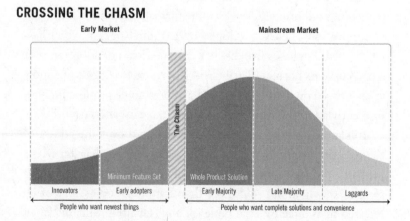

Early Market   Mainstream Market

The Chasm

Minimum Feature Set   Whole Product Solution

| Innovators | Early adopters | Early Majority | Late Majority | Laggards |

People who want newest things   People who want complete solutions and convenience

SCOTT: Geoffrey, the core of your book is illustrated on the front, which is this model that you talk about called the "technology adoption life cycle." There is, in a sense, five profiles, if you will, all with different psychographic differences. Let's start there so everybody has a bit of a working knowledge. Would you take maybe a minute or two on each of these five profiles and talk about why they're so important to understand in this technology life cycle?

GEOFFREY: Right, and just to give credit where credit is due to predecessors of mine, Everett Rogers actually did the original work on the technology adoption life cycle. He called it the "Diffusion of Innovation." And then I spent some time with a man named Regis McKenna, who really reinvented high-tech marketing in the 1980s. He was the one who brought the technology adoption life cycle into the tech market. My addition was this thing called "the chasm," which I'm sure we'll get to.

The key to the principle of this model is, when you introduce a disruptive innovation into any community, it will self-segregate into these five adoption profiles, each of which, as you've said, has a different psychographic.

The very first adopters, we call them the "technology enthusiasts." They are genuinely interested in technology for technology's sake. So, they will spend a lot of time with the technical team. They want to know how things work. They want to help in any way they can. They like to get beta copies, or even alpha copies of technology. They'll work with your bugs, etc. I always think of them as Sheldon on *Big Bang Theory*. It used to be Doc Brown from *Back to the Future*, but I'm dating myself.

That's that first profile. They don't have any money. They can't actually effect change, but what they do is they let everybody else in the community know whether this technology is real or not. Is this cold fusion or is this virtual reality? Where are we?

The second psychographic we call "the visionaries," and these are the people who make the first big bets on a disruptive innovation. They know they're going first. They know it's not done yet. They're willing to put a lot of project resources behind it. They're willing to put their own skin in the game, because their vision is, "If this technology does what I think it can do, it will change my industry and I will catapult myself to the top."

So, I'm Jeff Bezos. I'm going to completely reinvent the book distribution industry, and then consumer products, and then etc., etc., etc. Bezos is a classic visionary. Steve Jobs is a classic visionary. Larry Ellison, Bill Gates . . . all these guys were visionaries. They were first, and then they made dramatic changes.

Those two constituencies, however, are a minority of the population in any community. The majority of the population is made up with the next two profiles. We call them "the pragmatists" and "the conservatives."

The pragmatists are saying, "Look, this stuff is kind of amazing. It kind of works. It gets better as you go along. You don't want to be too early because you might back the wrong company and they may go out of business. There's a lot of risk, so keep your eyes sharp. Stay alert to the category, but don't really jump in until other people jump in, too."

It's kind of like a junior high dance problem. I'm going to dance when I see other people dancing. I don't want to be first, but also, I don't want to be last. So, stick with the herd with the pragmatist model, and be very pragmatic about it. You don't expect that the world's going to change in ninety days, but you want to make sure you get good value, and you want to manage things carefully. Set expectations, then meet expectations.

The fourth group are called "the conservatives," because they, by and large, don't get a lot of value from technology or disruptive innovations. They want to be late to the game. And by the time they get there, they want all the bugs gone. They're going to want to spend a little bit less than the pragmatists because the market is more mature. That's fine with them. Their biggest concern is not to be so late that they actually miss the party entirely, which means they're willing to wait longer than the pragmatists. They're a loyal member of the previous regime—they're still on Macintosh when you switch to Windows, and then they're on Windows when you switch back to Macintosh. But they're part of an installed base. Tech is taking this installed base and the churn much more seriously and offering services. So, the conservatives, who frankly were a neglected constituency in the era of product, have become a much more interesting constituency in the era of service.

And then the final group we called "the skeptics," and they just fundamentally think that technology is way overblown, way overvalued. So, they just want to get the cheapest, most minimal thing they can get.

The point about those five groups is that the way you sell to them, the way you support them, the way you engage with them, is very different. When you're bringing a technology to market for the first time, which is what *Crossing the Chasm* is about, you have to take them on in sequence. What that causes you to do is to have to change your strategy and even your whole approach as you go through that life cycle. That's very strange because you get really good at selling to one group, and all of a sudden, you've got to sell to the next one, and you've got to sell completely differently. And what they look for in your company is different. It's a challenge and that's where the *Crossing the Chasm* challenge came.

Too often, organizations sell to the early adopters and the early majority. And that marketplace is quite small and not as influential—these are people who will test and buy anything that comes out, and if you want to create a sustainable business, you must make sure you don't fall victim to the passion, the curiosity, the commitment, the loyalty, and the discretionary spending of these early customers, because you can get fooled by that. And then your market is over. To build a sustainable business, make sure you understand how to create what Geoffrey calls the "bandwagon effect" to move on to the next three psychographic profiles, which will be the majority of your buyers.

The bandwagon effect is well known in business and marketing to describe the phenomenon whereby people buy and do things simply because others are. There are countless examples of this effect in our lives, although I'm sure we all think we're savvy buyers and immune to marketing messaging (woe to the person who actually believes that's true about themselves).

But if we're honest, we could think of dozens, if not hundreds, of purchasing decisions made because we saw someone with something new. Why else would many star athletes and actors earn more in product endorsements than they do at their best-of-class craft? From teeth whiteners to bottled water, cosmetics, perfumes, and apparel—the proof of the bandwagon effect is indisputable. Ask me why my pantry is full of hundreds of Nespresso pods. Five words: Stephanie Miller loves George Clooney.

Understanding the chasm of your business is crucial to ensuring the marketplace of buyers is large enough and deep enough to build a sustainable future. I know of too many authors that get lured into thinking their book is going to be a massive success because all their friends have said they'll buy one. The challenge wasn't that their friends wouldn't buy it—they did. But that's where it stopped; that was their chasm and few ever cross it.

THE TRANSFORMATIONAL INSIGHT

Every business has a chasm. Your ability to create, ride, or build a bandwagon is a key differentiator from your competition—and perhaps the key to survival.

THE QUESTION

Have you paid the price to anticipate your chasm and build a strategy to cross it successfully?

JOEL PETERSON

FRANKLINCOVEY
ONLEADERSHIP
WITH SCOTT MILLER

EPISODE 99

JOEL PETERSON
ENTREPRENEURIAL LEADERSHIP

EVER MEET SOMEONE in life whose credentials and success are so extraordinary that your jealousy of them clouds your feelings for them? As in, you know you should like them and use them as a model for your own life but your insecurity around them is at times crippling? Or if not crippling, certainly debilitating. As in, you want to hate them but they're so kind and wise and their success is actually really deserved because of their work ethic and disciplined focus on high return activities?

Well, I've just described my relationship with Master Mentor #50, Joel Peterson.

Joel's professional resume reads like the bio of a U.S. president or senator. Let's take a stroll through parts of it. Brace yourself, your envy gene is about to get lit up. So I'll only touch on the highlights.

Joel earned his MBA from Harvard Business School. Then he went on to spend eighteen years working for what was once the largest real estate developer in the United States, the Trammell

Crow Company, where he rose to become its chief financial officer and managing partner. With appointments crossing the United States and Europe, Joel left Crow and founded Peterson Partners, Inc., a Utah-based private equity firm that has funded and ignited the growth of some of the brightest successes in entrepreneurial history including Bonobos, JetBlue Airways, Asurion, Madison Reed, Allbirds, Breeze Airways, Chatbooks, Ethos, Packsize, and countless others.

Concurrently, Joel began teaching business and leadership classes at the Stanford Graduate School of Business, where he's been an icon with students for thirty years. He's served on more than three dozen boards over the past forty-five years and until recently was the chairman of the board of JetBlue for twelve years. Joel also served as the chairman of the board of Overseers at the Hoover Institution, the prestigious public policy think tank that counts former Secretary of State Condoleezza Rice, Jerry Yang, and Rupert Murdoch among its members.

Along the way Joel made a few dollars. And gave many of them away to causes and foundations his family is dedicated to.

And in case you think Joel's done all of this at the expense of his family life, he has seven children, thirty-one grandchildren and has been married to his stunning, gracious, generous, classy, and sophisticated wife, Diana, for fifty years and counting. Look at the accomplishments of his children, and you'll see the apple hasn't fallen far from the tree.

Grrrr . . .

Of course, I meant to type "Great," but I swear the *r* key got stuck on my keyboard. Really, I wouldn't lie over such a minute thing (yes I would).

Joel has also authored several books including one I want to focus this chapter on, titled *Entrepreneurial Leadership*. In our podcast conversation, Joel describes what he terms "the six types of leaders," the last being the Entrepreneurial Leader—what he thinks all leaders should aspire toward. And Joel would know after fifty years leading companies himself as well as hiring and firing leaders across many industries. His words haunt me (in a good way) as I transition from a C-suite officer in a public company to now being the owner of my own albeit small but growing firm with full- and part-time employees and many contractors all reporting to me. I've inserted this portion of our interview so you can hear Joel directly in his own words.

SCOTT: What I'd like to do is open today's conversation talking about the five types of leaders that you illustrate in your book to set up a sixth type called the Entrepreneurial Leader. I'll pitch you the type and ask you if you'll give us a minute or so on each of these five types of leaders that you've come to recognize over your 50+ years in business. The first is the Presider. Talk a bit about the Presider.

JOEL: The Presider is somebody who maintains the status quo, who cuts ribbons, kisses babies, executes policy, keeps things moving forward. And I think it's quite valuable to have somebody as a leader who is a Presider. But it's not enough to adapt to the market, to hire great teams, to do all the things that the entrepreneurial leader needs to do. But I think it's one element that's important in a leader.

SCOTT: You could argue that there are certain phases of a business when a Presider might be just fine for a certain period of time, perhaps where the board or the founders are looking for the future leader to pivot for a new opportunity.

JOEL: Actually, I think when you're focused on maintaining stability, Presiders are great.

SCOTT: You call the second type of leader the Manager. Talk about that person.

JOEL: The Manager is the person who can deal with complexity. Managers are phenomenal. They can deal with all kinds of information, sort it out, put it in order, create processes, and manage the complexity.

SCOTT: The third type is the Administrator.

JOEL: Administrators are typically people who understand policy really well, the implications of policy and getting policy right. Policy is quite a powerful thing. And it sort of creates the framework within which businesses operate. So, great Administrators are really valuable.

SCOTT: And then, Joel, interestingly your fourth distinguishing leadership style, if you will, you call it the Pure Entrepreneur, which you would think might be about entrepreneurial leadership, but it's not. It's a different type of entrepreneur. Talk about the Pure Entrepreneur.

JOEL: There are a few people in our business world who are phenomenal at lighting fires. They have an idea a minute, they can create new things, and they're really valuable. But many of them have a hard time keeping the fire burning and turning it into something that is durable, where they can bring teams on or they bring their successor on. There's actually a concept called the "Founder's Trap" where founders start the company and then the trap is they can't take it to the next level. So, the Pure Entrepreneur is an innovator, a fire lighter.

SCOTT: And then lastly, the fifth one, the Politician.

JOEL: Politicians understand power. And they're really good at rewarding friends, punishing enemies, and getting things done through compromise. So, I think while Politicians have sort of a low rating in today's society, among many people they actually play quite a valuable safety valve role. And the same thing with leaders in organizations. There are some people who just understand the politics of an organization and they're able to move things through that would otherwise get gummed up.

SCOTT: And then, Joel, juxtapose these five types of leaders that you've encountered, you've hired, you've coached. Perhaps you've been some of these yourself. What are the key distinguishing characteristics between these five and the Entrepreneurial Leader?

JOEL: I think the Entrepreneurial Leader understands that all five are necessary. They don't necessarily have to be all five of them, but they have to bring onto their team and empower somebody who can do each of those five elements because you don't have complete leadership without all five being present.

I use the term *Five Tool Player*. People who know baseball are very aware that the Five Tool Player can run, throw, hit for power, hit for average, and field. They have to be able to do all five of those, and there are not many players (in the Major Leagues, even) who are great Five Tool Players. But when you have somebody who's a Five Tool Player, they become an All-Star, they become a Hall of Famer, and so the Entrepreneurial Leader is the same kind of Five Tool Player. They don't necessarily have to be able to do all of them themselves, like a baseball player does, but they have to appreciate them. Bring people on who can do them, empower them, celebrate them, and create a whole team.

SCOTT: As a private equity investor in hundreds of companies, you've founded a few, you've helped to sell a few, you've invested in 100+, some more successful than others. Talk to our listeners and viewers about when you coach a Pure Entrepreneur, like a founding entrepreneur, and you need them to move toward becoming an Entrepreneurial Leader. What types of coaching conversations do you have? They are probably high courage, where someone hasn't been able to move from one of these five exclusively to becoming a true Entrepreneurial Leader. What is that conversation like?

JOEL: Usually it has to do with things like bringing on a great team, identifying the areas where they're not strong, and filling them in with people who are phenomenal in a high trust environment where values are shared. Because business is a team sport, and if you don't create that team—and frankly, if the original entrepreneur doesn't understand where his or her weaknesses are, where their gaps are, they'll be reluctant to bring on great team members who can fill those gaps.

I remember Peter Drucker once telling me that my job was to understand where my weaknesses were, to build on my strengths, and fill in my weaknesses with other people. I think that's what the great Entrepreneurial Leader does: build a system around him or her that completes the picture of the Entrepreneurial Leader, and few people become all of them.

I actually list a couple of people in the book that surprise most readers. I list Alan Mulally who nobody thinks would be an Entrepreneurial Leader. He led Boeing, after all, and then Ford Motor Company, but he's really quite creative, quite innovative, quite able to manage a large organization. I also list Stan McChrystal, who is a four-star general, who dealt with the Special Operations Forces in our country. And he was quite entrepreneurial, he was able to knit them together in a way that really made a difference.

SCOTT: Joel, as an investor have there been times when you've invested in a Pure Entrepreneur because you felt like their skills at that point were extraordinary and their idea was great, but there came a time when it was clear to you—whether because you were on their board of directors, or you were an investor—that it was time for them to step aside, step out, step away, because they didn't have the right skills for the next phase of the business, and how has that gone? And how did they respond?

JOEL: Sure, that happens quite frequently. In fact, usually when you invest in a new business, you are really backing the entrepreneur, their energy, their creativity, and their ability to create something new. In many cases, the entrepreneur can't take it to the next level.

I think one case that everyone knows about is Steve Jobs who hit a wall at a certain point in time at Apple. He left, did some other things, and came back and was then actually quite successful at it. I think the founder of JetBlue is the same way. David Neeleman is the most brilliant entrepreneur I've ever worked with in terms of creating a new airline. But after early first phases of JetBlue, moving to the next phase was not up his power alley. He then went out and formed Azul, created a big success there and is back at creating new airlines again, and I think he's learned to become an Entrepreneurial Leader.

So, calling all Entrepreneurial Leaders: Joel Peterson has, with a bit of street cred, made it clear that each of us needs to understand our strengths and weaknesses and build complementary teams around us. At this point in the book, if you've done the work and discovery from Tasha Eurich's and Julian Treasure's chapters, you should be well on your way. However, if you phoned it in and thought my advice and instructions seemed lame, I strongly suggest you don't call Joel Peterson to fund your next venture. He'll save those dollars for someone who has strong self-awareness, knows their communication style, and has learned how to master all six of the styles, or at least has filled their gaps with others around them.

Whether that reads like an "Ouch" or an "Opportunity" is solely up to you.

. . .

THE TRANSFORMATIONAL INSIGHT

Even if you're not a traditional entrepreneur, successful leadership calls on you to demonstrate Entrepreneurial Leadership skills.

THE QUESTION

Which of the five Leadership Styles do you need to shore up to come into your full potential as an Entrepreneurial Leader?

GUY KAWASAKI

FRANKLINCOVEY
ONLEADERSHIP
WITH SCOTT MILLER

EPISODE 48

GUY KAWASAKI
A BUFFET OF GOOD ADVICE

GUY KAWASAKI IS the very definition of what wisdom sounds like. He's highly educated but plainly spoken. Enormously successful but humble and full of gratitude. In our *On Leadership* interview about his book *Wiseguy*, our discussion had so many insights it was hard to choose one for this chapter.

So I didn't choose one. In fact, I chose thirteen.

Unlike the other Master Mentors and Transformational Insights thus far, I've included multiple insights Guy shared, as I think they all hold the potential of being transformational without going deep into just one. Which means, in this chapter, take what you like, leave what you don't. But I anticipate that you'll find all of them, if not transformational, highly valuable.

A bit about Guy before you dive in: Guy has authored more than fifteen *New York Times* and *Wall Street Journal* bestselling books and currently hosts *Guy Kawasaki's Remarkable People* podcast (it's pure gold—you must subscribe). Guy is best known as one of the earliest Apple employees and has built a global reputation as a marketing expert and brand building phenom. He serves as an ambassador for many brands including Mercedes and Canva, and I'd best describe him as an energy infuser. Total joy and positivity even though, like many, he's been through a few fires and back. I highly recommend you follow Guy on his social platforms. Like Seth Godin, he offers a constant stream of wisdom all through an unstoppable abundance mentality.

Okay, now for the wealth of wisdom from Guy:

The Future Cost of Short-Term Kindness. Kindness isn't always the best approach. Especially in high-stakes conversations or when your courageous feedback could literally change someone's perspective—often about themselves.

Thank Those Who Helped You Before They're Gone. Every one of us can name the person (for me, multiple people) who altered our trajectory for the better. Call them up and tell them. Now. Before it's too late.

Good People Do Bad Things and Bad People Do Good Things. Judge people by the totality of their lives, contributions, behaviors, and decisions. It's easy and limiting to make judgments based on a single encounter. Would you want someone doing that to you?

Motivation for Motivation's Sake. Simply put, it doesn't matter what motivates you as long as you're motivated. Don't feel ashamed or less than others because of your motivations. Use whatever it takes to change your circumstance and move forward toward your goals.

Be Motivated by Other People's Success. It's easy to be intimidated by and jealous of others' success. In fact, it's natural as a human to have jealousies. Own it. Resist that natural reaction and instead let it inspire you to achieve the same or even more.

Don't Take Offense. Take the High Road. Give People the Benefit of the Doubt. It's the second of *The Four Agreements* by Don Miguel Ruiz: Don't Take Anything Personally. But don't go so far as to become "thick skinned" where nothing comes in, but sadly, nothing goes out, either. Rather, have transparent skin where stuff comes in and stuff goes out freely, as inspired to me by the incomparable talent, Viola Davis.

Once You Believe You're a Victim, You Will Truly Become a Victim. It's easier than we all think to fall into a victim mentality. That leads to also being a martyr and then it's all downhill from there.

In Many Cases It Takes Courage to Quit. Don't believe the phrase "Once a quitter always a quitter." That's nonsense. Sometimes quitting is absolutely the right thing to do. Quitting one thing to focus or start on another is how we align our talents and passions with what ultimately brings us joy. Hyrum Smith, FranklinCovey's cofounder, famously defined character as "the ability to carry out a worthy decision once the emotion of making that decision has passed." The key word here, people, is *worthy*.

Maybe the Pasture Isn't Always Greener. It's often referred to as "The Law of the Harvest." Sometimes we harvest too soon or even from the wrong plot. It might be best to keep watering, planting, fertilizing, and weeding. Harvesting is clearly more fun and rewarding but be sure your timing is right and you're on the right land. (By the way, that was a metaphor, people. Never been on a farm in my life—here come the heartland invitations via Instagram.)

Are You Trustworthy? Remember, you don't get to decide the answer. The other person gets to decide. Ask yourself, "Have I behaved myself into a reputation of being trusted by others?"

Changing Your Mind Is a Sign of Confidence and Intelligence.
Being open to influence with new facts, new ideas, and information is a sign of maturity, emotional agility, and nimbleness—not weakness.

In Life You Are Always Selling. Repeat after me. "Everyone is in sales. Even me. Especially me." Develop your communication, empathy, and listening talents to ensure your sales skills are top notch.

Your Exploitation May Be My Opportunity. Sometimes you have to spend money to make money. And when I say *money*, I also mean time and effort. You won't get paid for everything you do in life. The most successful people are always the most abundant and willing to make investments that don't always pay off. But those same people rarely feel exploited because their mindset is one of potential opportunity and not exploitation.

Any one of these, individually, can be transformational. If you find one in particular hits you square in the head, watch the *On Leadership* interview as Guy shares an endearing story about each concept that all of us can relate to. And the interview just might be what you need to take action. And for further wisdom from Guy, absolutely pick up a copy of his book, *Wiseguy*. It's a mine full of gold waiting to be discovered.

THE TRANSFORMATIONAL INSIGHT

Guy shares thirteen Transformational Insights. Grab your tray, load up your plates, and gorge to your heart's content.

THE QUESTION

How many trips can you make to the buffet line (Guy's wisdom)? This isn't like a real buffet where people will stare at you if you return more than once.

MICHAEL HYATT

FRANKLINCOVEY
ONLEADERSHIP
WITH SCOTT MILLER

EPISODE 74

MICHAEL HYATT
YOUR PRODUCTIVITY SYSTEM

You HAVE A productivity system. Whether you know it or not.

What's a productivity system? Ideally, it's the intentional integration of tools, print and digital, to help you leverage your time and maximize your productivity.

I'm often on cross-country flights and marvel at how many of us are doing one of two things: relaxing watching a movie or working deep within Outlook. Like most of humanity, I live much if not most of my working hours in Outlook. I write all my book chapters in email and then congeal them together in the publisher's final software program for copy editing. I check my Outlook schedule 15+ times a day as that's about the number of podcasts, calls, meetings, or scheduled projects I work on during a typical day. I perform nearly all my writing in Outlook, which includes blogs, articles, columns, requests for book endorsements, and quotes for news/media outlets.

Mission accomplished, Mr. Gates. You're welcome.

Perhaps it's me who should be thanking him. Although I've certainly contributed my share to Microsoft's coffers, they've enabled my productivity far beyond what I could have ever imagined. But even though I spend most of my waking hours in Outlook, I deliberately use it as a *component* of my overall productivity system, not my *complete* system. I, like billions of others, still use pen and paper for certain aspects of my day and I don't anticipate that changing.

What? Scott Jeffrey Miller still uses a paper planner?

Yep.

I also still write my handyman a check when he comes as neither of us have a Venmo account (although my wife is sadly a pro at all technologies that send money out the door).

Before you pass judgment that I'm a technological Luddite, I have a solid Instagram following, I post daily on four separate social platforms, I use Google Docs for many projects, and I engage on multiple Slack channels. I would have included turning on Netflix in that list, but because of the various parental controls and restrictions in place to protect our sons from certain programming, ironically, I have to ask said sons how to log in and bypass the very settings I set up in the first place.

How much deliberate thought have you invested into your productivity system? Have you intentionally designed an integrated system that works for you?

I can tell you I have, thanks in great part to Michael Hyatt, the multi-bestselling author whose Full Focus Planner I use daily.

Now you might be thinking, aren't you the FranklinCovey guy? Why aren't you using a Franklin Planner? Well, I have, for nearly three decades, and although that product is no longer associated with our company, the Franklin Planner is still a superb tool and I have enormous respect for their products and the people who design them. But it just so happens that after reading Michael's many books, I've come to find his particular tool ideal for where I am in my life as a parent, husband, and entrepreneur. I like his planning and goal-setting methodology and the actual, physical, printed tool matches my current style preference. I also suspect not everyone who works for GM drives only GM cars or those who work for Wendy's don't hit the Golden Arches on occasion. Or more radically, grab a taco.

So now that you're over my perceived lack of loyalty to the Franklin Planner, let's address the real elephant in the room: are paper planners even still a thing?

Um, yep.

Ask Michael Hyatt who sells thousands of them to people like me annually. Ask Franklin Planner. Ask Filofax. Ask Martha Stewart. Ask Daytimer. Ask Smythson. Ask the friend of a friend who will only use a particular brand of paper planner from Japan and orders them from the Land of the Rising Sun directly. Even though they're not in English and she can't read Japanese.

You might be pleasantly surprised and even validated to learn that many highly productive people choose either all digital, all paper, or a combination of both that results in an intentionally designed and integrated productivity system that works uniquely for them.

The key there is the phrase *for them*.

Mark Twain reportedly said, "The reports of my death are greatly exaggerated."

The same can be said about paper-based productivity systems whose demise has been wrongfully predicted for years. Millions of professionals a year still integrate a paper-based planning tool into their productivity system, like me, and perhaps you. The point is, there is no right or wrong productivity system, there is only the system that works for you and prompts consistent and effective use. If that means attaching sticky notes to your pet turtles, you be you.

Here's how my productivity system works:

I use my Full Focus Planner mainly to make my daily task lists, to keep notes from meetings, to deliver on promises made to others, and to capture my creative thoughts—four vitally important parts of my day and business. I use Outlook for all my appointments, contacts, and obviously email. If I was to track their use, it would likely be about 50/50 across any typical day. My Full Focus Planner travels with me whenever I leave my desk. It's in every restaurant. (I eat breakfast and lunch out seven days a week.) It's in every offsite meeting. It's always open during every Zoom/Teams meeting I'm on as that's how and where I write my notes and capture deliverables. Most vitally, it's my tool to make and keep promises—which hopefully is my brand.

Much of my wisdom has obviously come from my 26+ years working with FranklinCovey, an undisputed expert on personal productivity and time management, but Michael Hyatt has put some icing on the proverbial cake for me. His book, *Free to Focus: A Total Productivity System to Achieve More by Doing Less*, has accelerated my commitment to the integration of both print and digital tools into my life.

One of the biggest insights I've taken from studying Michael's productivity methodology is that our Productivity Systems should not be used accidentally to build a life that's out of balance. Being more productive shouldn't mean that you have less time for those activities and priorities that define your purpose, mission, and legacy. I'm learning to resist the trap that enhancing my productivity always equates to me working more and getting more done as a result. When Michael would argue, it's not about getting more done, it's about getting more of the *important* things done.

I've inserted a short excerpt from my *On Leadership* interview with Michael that illustrates this point:

SCOTT: Michael, your recent book is piercingly relevant. FranklinCovey has a couple of points of view, if you haven't noticed, on productivity. I really liked your opening concept about this idea of total work. Can you give a little bit of texture around why total work should be a concept that people are addressing and identifying in their lives?

MICHAEL: Yeah, we live in a world where it's kind of a badge of honor to be able to say, "Man, I'm crazy busy!" or "It's work all the time!" Somehow that gives us a sense of significance and importance. It's a very deceptive thing because, if we're not careful, we're going to end up burning out and not doing our best work.

One of the things in recent years is this concept I've come to identify as the "hustle fallacy" as it's particularly pernicious if you're really serious about getting ahead, if you want to advance your career, you want to build your business, then it's got to be total work. You got to be willing to put in eighty, ninety hours a week. Elon Musk has even advocated a hundred hours a week.

And I say hogwash.

In fact, that is a recipe for burnout. And I'm committed to what I call the double win, where you win at work and succeed in life. And I don't think we should have to choose between those two, because I think we can do them both if we have the right productivity system and the right priorities.

Just as with his planners, Michael knows that integration of the two seemingly disparate sectors of life can exist. Do you have to sacrifice your personal life for a successful career? No. Should you set all your dreams aside to live a life of leisure and relaxation? Also no. It's about the double win, getting both sides of your life to work together. And it becomes tactical as you implement and use a customized productivity system that works for you.

Your productivity system needs to address four key components: a place and process for calendaring, tasks, appointments, and notes. Once you've decided whether those are going to be supported through a digital tool, a paper tool, or an integrated process of both, be mindful of some of these planning pitfalls:

- Not being consistent with using your system.

- Not being clear on what's important to you.

- Not moving unresolved items to the next day.

- Not taking advantage of "secret" productivity tools that often come bundled with productivity software or platforms.

So take a moment and become intentional about your productivity system. If you're like most of us, there are a few things in your life that are keeping your day from being more streamlined and enjoyable and keeping you from finding your double win. Identify ways to integrate systems to better work for you. And remember that your solution may not be the same as your neighbor, friend, colleague, or spouse, and that's okay. It's all about what works for you and keeps you on your most productive track to avoid burnout and achieve what matters most . . . to you.

I've listed below some key points I think you should consider if you're integrating paper into your productivity system. The fact is, I work with hundreds of highly effective individuals across my many professional roles. And nearly every one of them combines digital and print as a harmonious system.

- **Resist at all costs the Comparison Conundrum.** Don't let the tech early adopter on the team overly influence your decisions. Their constant stream of new gadgets are likely more for show than productivity. Build what works for you. Trust me, they are watching you more than you're watching them.

- **Don't be afraid to switch systems or try new tools.** Because you bought a $49 planner in January doesn't mean you can't test a new one in April. Lean in to testing and trying different options to find what works best for you. Simply because you've only filled a quarter of the tool/planner/notebook, doesn't mean you can't (or shouldn't) pivot onto something better or different.

- **Practice some self-reflection on your tactile preferences.** Do you love using mechanical pencils? Roller ball vs fountain pens? Blue versus black ink? Is there a type, size, or design format of paper that inspires you and brings your energy and focus to life? Study and identify your own preferences and leverage them in your system.

- **Ensure you know the meeting, planning, scheduling, and communication culture of your employer** so your systems integrate and leverage the efficiencies of the organization. And if you're the leader or owner, you must also create an intentional culture around these to ensure alignment and collaboration.

- **Ask around for advice and options.** Exercise the confidence to poll those most effective around you about what their overall system looks like and determine which tools might work for you. Don't be surprised if their answer is underwhelming or surprisingly simple.

- **Remember, it's your system.** Don't let public opinion or current trends overly impact your design. Build, change, and leverage what works best for you. I write my monthly goals on a large chart pad and stick it to my office wall so I look at them all day long. This might seem old school or absurd to some, but it works for me (as evidenced by all the lines drawn through the goals) and that's what really matters: Goals accomplished! Yes, I draw lines through my completed goals, not check marks as it's much more satisfying!

- **Think about your whole life—all your roles—including what your life looks like on the weekends and during non-work time.** Does your system allow you to achieve the balance and productivity you want and need? Develop a system that hooks into every aspect and element of your life. We have many roles that we play, and you don't want your tool to become obsolete at the end of your workday and then find yourself always catching up, overwhelmed, or compromised in the most important non-work areas of your life.

- **Be gentle on yourself.** Your system didn't work last week like you hoped? Try again. You stayed true to it for three days but lagged on two? Try again. Like all systems, yours will work for or against you based on your willingness to adapt and improve. Perhaps 30 percent, 50 percent, or 75 percent adoption is a major win for you. Be proud of your progress and keep your momentum going.

- **Along with the flexibility you're allowing yourself around your choice of tool, your own discipline is an equal and necessary investment to create the life you want.** Your productivity system's impact may be minimally used as a support tool or a fully navigating compass and engine, but you must establish the cadence and commitment to make it work . . . for you.

- **Most of all, make it fun.** Somewhere along the way somebody with a stick up their you-know-what sucked the fun out of work and perpetrated this myth that smart, productive people can't also have fun. Buy or create your system that's energizing and motivates you! Stickers are in vogue!

. . .

THE TRANSFORMATIONAL INSIGHT

Choosing your productivity system should be done intentionally and deliberately to ensure you achieve the double win in life.

THE QUESTION

Are you able to resist the latest fads and simply lean in to what works for you?

JULIE MORGENSTERN

FRANKLINCOVEY
ONLEADERSHIP
WITH SCOTT MILLER

EPISODE 38

JULIE MORGENSTERN
TIME TO PARENT

For those of you who know a bit about me, you are likely aware that I am what I would describe as a reluctant parent. I got married later in life at the age of forty-one. I never really wanted to get married or have children.

Wait, let me say that differently.

I most *definitely* did not want to have children. But then as with all great love affairs, I met a smart and beautiful girl in a gym, and next thing I knew, I was married and had three sons in five years.

Don't do that. Meaning, maybe get married, but don't have three kids in five years—I highly *don't* recommend that. At the time of this writing, my wife and I are blessed (at least that's what I feel like I should say) to have three boys who are seven, ten, and twelve, and to my wife's absolute horror, they each have my indefatigable energy. So you can imagine what it's like in Millerland. (By the way, both of our dogs are also boys, so the male to female ratio is 6:1, mitigated by designer purses and jewelry to ensure she stays around.)

Like any parent, I've wanted to wave the white flag at times. But instead, wisdom always prevails, and I buy a parenting book to figure out how I can make sense of the mystery and chaos that is parenting. So I've read more than a few. And of all of the parenting books I've consumed, Julie Morgenstern's is my hands down favorite. Perhaps because she's a well-known and renowned expert on productivity, time management, and life organization—all of which parenting demands in abundance. She hit the nail on the head by writing a phenomenal book called *Time to Parent: Organizing Your Life to Bring Out the Best in Your Child and You.*

When I interviewed her, I was absolutely captivated. She presented a fairly typical grid known in the consulting world as the four-box model, where every organization's problems and opportunities can be mapped onto an X and Y axis. In the following transcript from our podcast interview, Julie describes a key challenge parents face: how you provide your children with everything they need but *don't* see—such as scheduling orthodontia appointments, buying their vitamins, parent-teacher conferences, registering for summer camp, etc.—with all the things they *do* see and appreciate—playing games, reading, trips to the park, etc.—which is the time you spend with them.

I'll expand on Julie's transformational insight aimed primarily at parents and caregivers of minor children. As I've done for every Master Mentor in this book, I've inserted a QR code at the end of the chapter so you can watch her interview. For those of you who want to bring sanity to your world as a parent, I highly recommend watching the full interview with Julie.

SCOTT: Julie, you can imagine with three young boys that I read a lot of parenting books, as does my wife, Stephanie. This one that you've written, *Time to Parent*, is enormously practical.

One of my favorite parts of the book is where you describe this concept you call the "parenting time matrix." What I'm going to ask my producers to do is to take you off video for a moment and put up this matrix and have you talk us through its impact on parents. I found it's exponentially helpful—not just the time matrix itself, but the understanding of when I'm in the adult world, when I'm in the child's world, and when I'm in the visible and invisible worlds. Would you take a few minutes to walk through why this is so valuable to so many people reading the book?

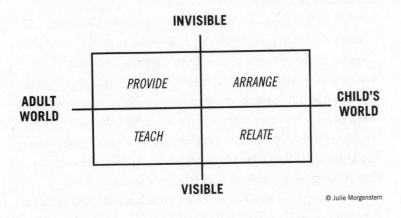

© Julie Morgenstern

JULIE: Parenting is the ultimate juggling act, and we, as parents, have to juggle a variety of responsibilities to take care of and raise kids. For us, we may have strengths in some areas or weaknesses in others, and it's very helpful to recognize that the different kinds of time that we spend as parents are perceived very differently by our children. It's not all the same.

So, I broke down the four things that we, as parents, must do.

We have to **provide** for our kids. We make money, work, pay for things.

We have to **arrange** the logistics of our kids' lives. Where do they go to school? What are they eating for lunch? How are they getting home? What do we do on the weekend?

We have to **relate** to our kids, which is getting to know them as the unique individuals they are.

And we have to **teach** our kids life skills and values so that they can survive and thrive out in the world.

While they all may feel like the same work to us, kids feel them differently. I always—both as a parent, as a coach, and working with parents—wondered about this very frequent phenomenon where you have parents who say, "I sacrificed my entire life for my kids," and those same kids will say, "My parents were never there for me."

How can that be?

Well, that's because some of the things we do for our kids take place in the adult world; some take place in the child's world. Some of them are visible to our kids, and some of them are invisible. And being aware of the distinction between those enables us to take care of our kids in a balanced way that communicates visibly to our kids how important they are to us.

You can see in the matrix that "provide" takes place in the adult world but it's largely invisible to our kids. They don't see us at work, they just know we're away working.

"Arranging" takes place in our child's world. You're doing stuff for your kids. They have a lunch packed, they get to school on time, they have clean clothes. But when are we doing that arranging? It's not visible to our kids. Mostly, it's at night after they go to sleep or when they're at school. They don't see the work.

"Relate" and "teach" are both visible. This is where we have that power. If you want to communicate to your kids that they are important to you, then you must spend time in "relate" and "teach."

But also recognize this—and I think for us as parents, this is a profound insight to absorb—teaching and relating feel different to our kids. Why? Because when we teach our kids, we are bringing them into the adult world. We're in charge of the agenda. We're talking about teaching them things that we feel are important for them, and they are our students. But, when we relate to our kids, when we get to know who they are, the unique people that they are, we have to actually enter the child's world and we become the student of the child.

They're very different, and as parents it's so easy to always teach. And we do that out of love, but we have to make sure that we are spending time relating in order to even teach. Kids aren't going to listen to you if they don't feel you understand them.

Those distinctions can help you navigate and balance your time appropriately. We need to do all four, but they're not all the same. The matrix enables us to be conscious of where we gravitate, the things we avoid, and make sure that we are touching all four bases.

For me, the most haunting takeaway of Julie's interview was what parents said after many coaching sessions: "I sacrificed my entire life for my kids," and those same kids will say, "My parents were never there for me."

For everyone reading this who is a parent, caretaker, guardian, aunt, uncle, neighbor, coach, teacher, or friend, how can we avoid this conundrum later in life?

The word choice that Julie uses around "adult world" and "child's world," "providing" and "arranging," "visible" and "invisible" has made me much more mindful and conscious of where I'm balancing my time.

Aware of Julie's categories, I've become hypervigilant of when I am operating in the adult world versus operating in my child's world and trying to implement small habits, like not bringing my phone into my son's basketball games. Or when one of my sons walks into my office and asks me a question, I put my phone down or turn away from my laptop, look him in the eye, and give him my undivided attention, even if it's just for thirty seconds.

Conversely, when I'm operating in the adult world or doing things that might be invisible for my children, I tell them that. When I walk in the door and my boys ask me how my day was, I will often tell them the things I worked on, including the things I did for them. Not to shame them, but to remind them that part of my day was spent doing things for them, which they otherwise may not fully be aware of. For example, I might say, "I spent twenty minutes on the phone with the dentist today, because it's important we have our teeth cleaned so we don't have any cavities. Later in life, you're not going to want to have a root canal." Now, again, it's hard for a ten-year-old to appreciate that, but they hear me more than I probably think they do.

Certainly, you have your own experiences, successes, and failures with these types of things. So, my intent with including Julie as a Master Mentor was to merely remind us parents and caregivers that we can find big wins in small things, that we should be mindful of when we're operating in the adult world versus the child's world, and that we should balance when we are taking on tasks that are invisible or visible.

. . .

THE TRANSFORMATIONAL INSIGHT

Parents and children live in different worlds. A child's ability to move into an adult's world is minimal. To be an effective parent or caregiver, you must move into theirs—and choose how to balance your time between the things they don't see (providing and arranging) with what they do see (teaching and relating).

THE QUESTION

If you were to track the time you spend in the adult world versus your child's world, what would your percentage be? What would your child's perception be? What should it be? What will it be?

DAVID SIBBET

FRANKLINCOVEY
ONLEADERSHIP
WITH SCOTT MILLER

EPISODE 20

DAVID SIBBET
VISUAL COMMUNICATION

THIRTY YEARS AGO, when I started my professional journey with the Disney Development Company, I had a career defining experience. More on that in a moment.

Up until then, I'd worked in a variety of roles including six in the restaurant industry, two as a real estate agent, and on numerous political campaigns at the local, state, and national levels. Fortunately, I learned that politics would become my avocation and not my vocation. It's an exhilarating, dirty business, and three decades later it's even worse.

Back to Disney.

I was very fortunate early in life to land a role at a Fortune 100 company working with a group of extraordinarily talented people, nearly all of whom had earned graduate business degrees and most from Ivy League schools. Want to destroy your self-esteem and self-confidence? Work with fifty people who all talk (with and without guile) about their Stanford, Harvard, Wharton, or

Columbia professors. At that point in my education, I was in transition from a local community college to our hometown private school, Rollins College, and I couldn't even tell you where Wharton was. In fact, the only Wharton I knew of was named Edith and her books were snoozers (admittedly, I may not be her target audience).

On the positive side, proximity to all these well-educated and intelligent people stretched and prompted me to build my skills, curiosity, and business acumen. Up until that point, my only business class in school, as an organizational communications major, was macroeconomics. To this day I still get the micro and macro thing mixed up and yet, perhaps shockingly, manage to keep paying the bills. Statistics, as you might imagine, was even worse.

Okay, about the defining experience . . . one day I was sitting in my cubicle, sweating my very existence in the company, working on a presentation around funding or some other project for my leader. Like me, they hadn't hailed from a prestigious school and needed help building a compelling business case. I was working on the slides and determined we should bring the numbers to life in a story or illustration of some type. I'd seen it done many times in the company by others, but I just didn't know how or where to start. So, I summoned an unnatural level of courage and walked over to the summer intern—yep, the intern from some super-duper expensive school—and asked if he could help me think through the illustration. I explained our vision, and within seconds, he was sketching out multiple ways it could come to life. To be clear, he wasn't an artist or even a creative type—he was just trained to bring numbers and financials to life in an illustrative format. He'd taken courses in business case planning and how to create pitch decks for venture capital firms, etc.

He handed me my options and as he stood up, I asked him where he'd learned how to do this, and I recall his response as if it were this morning: "Practice." And he then walked back to his cube, likely to dwell on his crushing student loan debt. Plus, his pants were too short. (Yes, I was riddled with crippling jealousy of his business skills and apparently it's lingered some.)

From that day thirty years ago, I've noticed a differentiating skill in professionals—the ability to competently illustrate their thoughts in ways that influence others.

Let's call it Visual Communication.

Fortunately, I know the world's expert on this competency, and it's Master Mentor #54, David Sibbet. I like to refer to David as the godfather of business illustration.

Ever been to a large conference and behind the keynote speaker on stage is a demure, quiet person swiftly capturing their genius words on some sort of banner in a remarkable feat of pictures and integrated images? Literally in real time as the speaker is imparting their genius (or pablum)? The artist is drawing what they're saying in a way that memorializes their words later to be displayed publicly for all to see. It's a remarkable and thus sometimes distracting talent that David Sibbet made popular and trained thousands of others in through his company, The Grove Consultants. David has authored/illustrated a series of compelling books including *Visual Meetings*, *Visual Leadership*, and *Visual Consulting* among others. These three are must-owns by anyone in business who wants to improve their credibility by bringing their thoughts (and the thoughts of others) to life in a clear and visually engaging way.

Why is this such an important competency? Let's look at my own career.

I'd consider my professional journey to have been exceptional by many standards, the macro/micro thing notwithstanding. But, and this is a big but, if there was one skill I wished I'd mastered it's the ability to stand in front of a gathering of people and transfer my verbal strengths onto the whiteboard, chart pad, or other perhaps digital capture system. Candidly, my credibility plummets when I'm handed a marker. Not only is my penmanship barely legible on paper, but it's also completely indecipherable when I'm trying to illustrate or capture group thoughts/comments in real time. Hell, I look crazed in normal times, let alone trying to speak and illustrate simultaneously. Which is why after thousands of meetings over the years, even though I was often the most junior person in the room early on, I was rarely nominated to capture the team's thoughts on the chart pad (known in the corporate world as paying your dues at the board).

It's a skill and I lack it.

Now to be serious, who really wants to be nominated to stand up in front of thirty colleagues at your CEO's ten-hour offsite and have to finally listen to every word said by everyone and also suddenly become an expert speller? Because there ain't nothing more embarrassing than standing in front of your peers and leaders wondering how to spell "superfluous."

How on earth would I check CNN every thirty minutes, search for "pet friendly hotels in Sarasota" and keep looking at my Delta app to see if I've been upgraded on my can't-come-too-soon flight home while I'm stuck at the front with a marker in my hand?

Been there?

No?

Liar.

And then there's that rare and annoyingly competent colleague of yours (who also never gossips, has a credit score of 810, two commas in their 401(k), and always seems to be onstage in Fiji at the Chairman's Club annual awards trip) who effortlessly walks up to the front of the room and knows all the tricks: what to capture and what not; when to use bullet points versus numbers; when to pull information into a Venn diagram; and all with the penmanship that would make an abbey of eighth-century monks green with envy.

These visual maestros do their work with a remarkable calmness, even when the meeting has descended into an episode of

Crossfire complete with screaming jerks (yes, jerks). They somehow manage to keep it all together while demonstrating the same confidence and aplomb when offering an idea of their own. Sometimes it boils down to raw talent. More likely, they have a system for how they organize complex ideas and present them visually.

I am jealous of these colleagues because they are some of the most influential people inside organizations. Fortunately, we can be taught such a system by David Sibbet.

David teaches a very simple formula he calls The Seven Basic Figures and The Seven Frames. I mastered them (a gross exaggeration) a decade ago when I started reading his books and I use his tools almost daily to slightly lift my credibility when I'm presenting. To clarify, my creativity in life vanished the moment my pen hit the paper, but these figures and frames from David can potentially transform your credibility, including my own.

I've included the key points from David that you could begin implementing immediately. Also included is a short explanation of when you might employ them based on the information you're trying to visually communicate. I implore you to read his books, consider taking some of his classes (thegrove.com) and minimally, watch our *On Leadership* podcast interview where he teaches many of these concepts on screen during our conversation.

The Seven Basic Figures. These are somewhat self-explanatory, but you're invited to study them more in-depth by watching David demonstrate their use and purpose in the video interview.

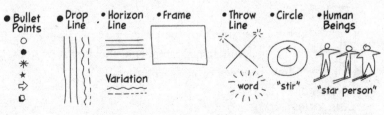

© David Sibbet

The Seven Basic Frames.

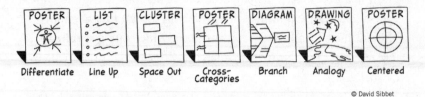

Differentiate

The Poster. Use the Poster Frame to focus attention on a single idea in order to differentiate it from others.

Line Up

The List. Use the List Frame to line items up and energize flow.

Space Out

The Cluster. Use the Cluster Frame to space out the information and invite comparison.

Cross-Categories

The Grid. Use the Grid Frame to build comparison across categories, showing how items compare or build on others.

Branch

The Diagram. Use the Diagram Frame to illustrate process or grow understanding through branching patterns.

Analogy

The Drawing. Use the Drawing Frame to animate meaning via a metaphor, story, or analogy.

Centered

The Mandala. Use the Mandala Frame to show an archetypal shape or pattern that everybody knows to organize information (such as a circle that unifies ideas).

Everyone can benefit from improving their Visual Communication skills, from building a quiver of options that allow you to better organize and contextualize information, to actually drawing pictures and storylines that help create momentum and capture the energy and direction of the conversation. It's not a question of *if* you're going to be handed the marker. Oh, you will be. The question is, *what* are you going to do with it, and will it build or diminish your credibility? Because it will either do one or the other based on your preparation, or as the Disney intern still making student loan payments would advise, "Practice."

Whether you use David's Figures and Frames (which I highly recommend as I think it's the best in the industry), you absolutely need to increase your confidence and credibility when it comes to illustrating ideas—yours or the CEO's.

. . .

THE TRANSFORMATIONAL INSIGHT

When your moment comes (and it will), your Visual Communication skills will be on display, impacting your credibility for your brand benefit or detriment.

THE QUESTION

How and when will you put in the practice to master the Seven Figures and Seven Frames?

LEENA RINNE

FRANKLINCOVEY
ONLEADERSHIP
WITH SCOTT MILLER

EPISODE 17

LEENA RINNE
LEARN THE HIDDEN STORY

You can't escape the current focus on empathy—books about the empathic leader, learning to be an empath, engaging in empathic listening.

It's everywhere.

As it should be.

It's the leadership competency that might stem the outflow of talent from your team or organization. We know the adage, people don't quit their job, they quit bad bosses and corrupt cultures. The Great Comeuppance, as I've named it, has hit every company worldwide.

Recently I was at lunch with a friend, and he is in in the midst of a career change and looking for, at the age of fifty-nine, what will likely become the crescendo of his professional life. Not the end, the crescendo, as it might be ten or fifteen years long. But he wants it to be meaningful and purpose-driven. We were talking about how, in his most recent role, he had four leaders in five years, all in the same division. His role didn't change but his leaders did, annually.

This friend currently works in higher education and was describing one leader in particular—someone who'd left a very prestigious private university, moved across the country, joined a large state university, and was immensely qualified for their leadership role.

On paper.

But their tenure in this new role was barely twelve months, as they wreaked havoc on the team. Classic case of high IQ and low—or no—EQ. The amount of empathy for people's challenges, points of view, backgrounds, feelings, and experiences was near zero. Highly competent, yet relieved of their role in a year because of their inability to build a high-trust team engaged in clear and valuable goals where people felt cared about.

Let me be unambiguous about this point: empathy is a leadership competency.

And it doesn't need to be taught as nearly everyone (unless you're a psychopath) has it. It just needs to be ignited and elevated as a skill vital to leading a team. So let's be clear on the definition: empathy is the ability to identify with and understand another's situation or feelings. It's a validation of someone else's truth or point of view. Keep in mind you can validate someone *without* agreeing with them (solid marriage and relationship advice right there).

Which brings us to Master Mentor #59, Leena Rinne. Leena is a seventeen-year associate at FranklinCovey and serves as our vice president of consulting. Fancy title—lots of responsibility. Ultimately, Leena is responsible for the talent and skill that every FranklinCovey consultant worldwide possesses and deploys with our clients, hundreds of times a day, globally.

Not a big deal—just the lifeblood of our company and brand.

Her bio will either inspire you or depress you depending on where your self-confidence sits. Leena is the two-time *Wall Street Journal* bestselling coauthor of *The 5 Choices: The Path to*

Extraordinary Productivity and *Fierce Loyalty: Cracking the Code to Customer Devotion*. She earned a masters in economics, is raising twin tween girls with her husband, fronts a rock band here in Salt Lake City, and frequently serves as a mentor to many on how to build a real estate empire with apartment rentals, as she and her husband Dave have done.

Born in Finland, but raised and educated in the United States, she has traveled the world delivering FranklinCovey's solutions to thousands of our clients. It's also common for me to text Leena to ask her a quick question and her response will be, "Just boarded a plane for Uzbekistan. No cell service—send email—will check in 9 hours." Or "I'm in Cabo for the wknd—stand by—will call after we filet our catch." Seriously, my last adventure was taking the garbage cans out in the snow and Leena's was likely hiking the Appalachian Trail with record speed and fun. And not to oversell her as a Master Mentor, but Leena is also a kind human being, full of abundance, and oh yeah, also rides a badass motorcycle.

Okay, I'll stop.

Leena coauthored the bestseller *Leading Loyalty* with Franklin-Covey colleagues Sandy Rogers and Shawn Moon from our Customer Loyalty practice. They've gained quite a following with leaders looking to differentiate their value proposition through loyalty with clients and internal associates alike. In the book and related course, Leena and her coauthors identify three Core Loyalty Principles that every organization should practice and use to guide their efforts: Empathy, Responsibility, and Generosity. Further, participants in the one-day work session learn how to lead and facilitate eleven "Huddles" with their team members that are crucial to instilling loyalty across the culture. They are:

Huddle 1   Loyalty Leader Mindset

Huddle 2   The Need for Empathy

Now, if any of those pique your interest, visit franklincovey.com to learn more about our Leading Loyalty solution. The one I want to elevate to a Transformational Insight is Huddle #4, which by necessity requires empathy as the starting point: Listen to Learn the Hidden Story.

Here's the deal . . . even if you've dissed me on all the other videos, I insist, I demand, I *command* you to watch the following video, titled *The Hidden Story*. I stake my reputation that you will appreciate this video:

Does this even need a debrief? Doubt it.

Okay—video time again.

As the famed author and psychologist Dr. Brené Brown has said, "Empathy is a choice, and it's a vulnerable one. Empathy fuels connection. Sympathy drives disconnection."

Empathy and sympathy are often used interchangeably. But they're not so similar. Have you seen the video on YouTube created by Brené to illustrate this? It's short and superb. Scan the QR code below to watch it. It's less than three minutes and well worth your time.

Two videos in a row that don't need a debrief . . . I'd say that's about as clear-cut as it gets.

Now apply the two videos to the goal of listening to learn the hidden story of others. Begin with the premise that everyone has a story, often not shared, but that's central to their experience, urgent for them in the moment, or even tied to their identity. Your goal is to apply empathy, resisting the urge, as Brené so well illustrates, to respond with, "At least . . ." and instead, listen without worrying or thinking about how to answer. Operationalized as a huddle often taught by Leena, a leader's best practices include:

- Asking simple, friendly, open-ended questions
- Staying silent until the person has finished talking
- Listening with your ears, eyes, and heart
- Not worrying about how to answer

Use empathy as the building blocks of trust in order to open yourself to the hidden stories of others. As a result, you'll not only be a better leader but a better human.

. . .

THE TRANSFORMATIONAL INSIGHT

Everyone has a hidden story. Invest in learning it.

THE QUESTION

For whom will you summon the patience, empathy, and interest to learn their hidden story and then determine how best to support them next?

JON HUNTSMAN JR.

FRANKLINCOVEY
ONLEADERSHIP
WITH SCOTT MILLER

EPISODE 143

JON HUNTSMAN JR.
HARD WORK STILL MATTERS

WHEN YOU AUTHOR a book, it's vital to understand that your publisher provides three main services. They:

Edit your manuscript.
Print your manuscript.
Distribute your manuscript.

Pretty much everything else is your responsibility. Yep, more than 90 percent of launching any book is the responsibility of the author.

Sobering? Yes.

Disappointing? Maybe, if you're a novice to the process.

Accurate? Oh, hell yes!

Over the past three years, I've authored five books (with four more in the near horizon) and resultingly, I've been privileged to be a guest on more than three hundred podcast, radio, and television programs as part of the launch strategy for each of them. For the record, it's measurably easier and more fun to be the guest than the host (and I've got some cred on both sides of the microphone).

Sidenote: For those of you looking to up your podcast game, either as a host or a guest, check out PodMatch.com. It's kind of like match.com, but for podcasters. And instead of finding a date, you find a host or a guest. I highly recommend it.

When I launched *Master Mentors Volume 1*, I made the rounds to nearly 150 podcasts, each of which I am grateful to for giving me a platform and for shining their light, some brighter than others, on my book. One of them, however, stands out from the rest. Stand by for that story.

A common question I'm asked by the host or interviewer is "What's the red thread that ties all the Mentors together?" To be completely truthful and transparent, there isn't one. Purposefully. I very much liked the idea of spotlighting mentors from different backgrounds and experiences, successes, and failures. So much so that one of my longstanding publishers—who is otherwise very bullish on my writing, brand, and future—passed on the book. They thought it was "too episodic." That it needed a common "red thread" or it would flop. I disagreed and talked with Harper-Collins Leadership, who caught my vision and jumped onboard. The *Master Mentors* series has performed exceptionally well, and I've also signed multiple deals with foreign publishers. I feel a bit vindicated/validated. (I talked with the first publisher who passed on the manuscript recently, and let's just say they wished they'd trusted my vision on this one.)

But the more I've thought about the red thread or through line that connects the thirty Master Mentors from the first volume and the second thirty from this volume, I've dug deeper, as the question keeps coming up. One commonality is clear—a requirement to be featured in the book was that you appeared on the podcast and had a Transformational Insight to share. Then beyond that commonality I saw in everyone an Abundance

Mentality, as our co-founder Dr. Stephen R. Covey called it. A generosity to lift others, share ideas, and exercise an uncommon level of vulnerability to invite others to learn from their pitfalls and even failures.

Then I discovered a third commonality: an indefatigable work ethic.

All the Master Mentors work extremely hard. And when they achieve a level of success and influence that most of us can't relate to, they don't just rest on their laurels. They double down. Then triple down. And then share those insights and successes with countless people around them.

Recently a podcast host asked me the "red-thread" question again, and armed with my third commonality I proceeded to respond. Only this time the host took offense (his word, not mine) at my suggestion that hard work was the key to success and becoming a Master Mentor. In fact, he was so offended by my suggestion that he revisited the point three times during our short interview. I didn't back off, because I genuinely believe the principle of "hard work" is a skill set. "Work smarter not harder" is a common refrain we hear. Sign me up for less work. Unless you want to make a significant contribution, impact, and influence on a large swath of people.

Since that interview (interrogation), I've revisited the through line of the first sixty Master Mentors and all 250+ of the *On Leadership* podcast guests and challenged the hard work premise. Was there a deeper commonality all or some of the mentors shared? As far as I can tell, hard work is it. Maybe something else will arise at some point, but I know hard work is definitely part of the Master Mentor calculation and formula for success. John Maxwell, Doris Kearns Goodwin, Seth Godin, Anne Chow, Emmanuel Acho, Jon Gordon, Jack Canfield, Matthew McConaughey, John Grey, Jamie Kern Lima, Patrick Bet-David, Mel Robbins, Arianna Huffington, Dr. Daniel Amen, Deepak Chopra, and Ryan Serhant, to name a few, are people I've come to know, some better than others. And despite their disparate fields of expertise, they all share an indefatigable work ethic. Period.

They outwork everyone I know.

They get up earlier.

They often schedule their days in fifteen-minute increments.

They make high-value decisions on where they marshal their energy, intellectual and physical.

And the list goes on. So I'm going to add another name to the previous list because I think coming with a certain family name and heritage carries with it an assumption that hard work, while admirable, had been largely displaced by serendipity.

Folks, to be a Master Mentor, that just ain't true. And it's certainly not the case for Jon Huntsman Jr., who I'd put at the top of that hard work list.

Does the name sound familiar? It's hard to know which honorific to use when addressing Jon, as his selfless service to the United States and the world is multifaceted. Jon has served as a three-time ambassador: to Singapore, China, and Russia. He is a two-time governor of Utah, my state of residence. He campaigned for the Republication nomination for U.S. President in 2012 and has since become a member of the boards of directors for Chevron and Ford.

Early in Jon's career, he was a staff assistant to President Ronald Reagan, deputy assistant secretary of commerce for President George H. W. Bush (41) and U.S. trade representative for George W. Bush (43). In case you think I've only highlighted him for his Republican leanings, you'd be mistaken as one of his diplomatic appointments was by a Democratic president, Barack Obama.

Now you may wonder why I've chosen to highlight a public servant and politician as the model of hard work among countless luminaries and entrepreneurs who've appeared on our podcast. Well, Jon's story is an interesting one. Tactlessly, a quick Google search of "what is Jon Huntsman Jr.'s net worth" returns the $1B result.

Yes, that was a B. (Forgive me Jon, I promise I'm going somewhere with this . . . trust me.)

Jon is the namesake of his late father Jon Huntsman, who was a legendary entrepreneur, philanthropist, and the founder of the former Huntsman Corporation, a massive petrochemical firm that pioneered much of the packaging you experienced at your local fast-food restaurants in the eighties.

What many may not know is that Jon began his career working in the family business. Not in some glamorous position as the founder's son, but in the trenches, doing the dirty work for many years right alongside other family members and company associates. Given his family's eventual success and extraordinary wealth, Jon easily could have skated like many socialites and trust funders.

Not even close.

Jon is truly one of the hardest working people I know. The man's dedication to his family, friends, community, foundations, corporate boards, and other ventures is not just admirable, it's invigorating.

From our *On Leadership* interview, Jon shared he grew up in a San Fernando neighborhood where everyone lived in a similar house, drove a Buick, and attended public schools. Jon's father worked in the chicken egg business, and some of Jon's earliest memories were traveling with his dad to talk to customers (learning early that no matter the business, the customer is king). Later they grew a small company and looked to purchase a manufacturing plant in Ohio. Although they had no money to buy the plant, the owner, Shell Chemical, was looking to largely give it away and so financed it for them. In the 1980s when they began manufacturing polystyrene, they had only five customers and were always at risk of losing one of them to a larger provider. Doing all the work was a trio of employees: Jon, his brother, and his dad. Jon worked on the production line as needed and the company came close to bankruptcy, or what they called "hitting the wall," multiple times.

Jon was no stranger to hard work. At fifteen he was a dishwasher, prep cook, and busboy at a Japanese restaurant. He dropped out of high school to play keyboards in a band called *Wizard* in 1978 (of course a band in 1978 was called "Wizard"), but worked hard to earn his way into the University of Utah and went on to graduate from the University of Pennsylvania. Jon served a two-year service mission for his church and learned to speak Mandarin Chinese and Taiwanese Hokkien.

Trust fund baby? Nope.

A relentless work ethic? Absolutely. It's the secret/not-so-secret sauce that underlies each Master Mentor I highlight and should be a core value to whatever pursuit in life you want to actually win at.

At the risk of someone dismissing the value of hard work as a Transformational Insight, I want to expand further on why I chose to highlight this quality in Ambassador Huntsman. Sometimes in life it's the simplest principles that have the most profound impact on our success. As I look back at the commonality of the Master Mentors spotlighted in this volume, including those in the first volume, as well as the 250+ guests on the podcast, I've become increasingly convinced that what they all share is a work ethic that differentiates them from those still striving, or in some cases cheating, their way to perceived success. Call me old-fashioned, but no amount of education, connections, money, charm, intellect, or charisma can replace the reputation and results that come from simply doing the work. That of course does not guarantee success to everyone just because they work hard. But I don't know anybody worth emulation who achieved success without hard work. As the old Irish saying goes, "You'll never plow a field by turning it over in your mind."

THE TRANSFORMATIONAL INSIGHT

In a world where the path of least resistance is an increasingly appealing option, working hard is a consistently safe bet for engineering a successful life.

THE QUESTION

Reflect on your successes and failures in life and privately correlate how your work ethic contributed.

MARTIN LINDSTROM

FRANKLINCOVEY
ONLEADERSHIP
WITH SCOTT MILLER

EPISODE 183

MARTIN LINDSTROM
UNCOMMON SENSE

I'VE WRITTEN ABOUT this before, but one of the most fortunate investments FranklinCovey made in me was that as an executive officer for over a decade, the CEO would fund the executive team's and other senior leaders' tuition to the annual World Business Forum. The event features two days of ongoing speeches from former prime ministers, presidents, business titans, Nobel Prize winners, and others with consequential ideas and research.

Of the ten years I attended and across hundreds of speakers, the one I remember the most profoundly was Martin Lindstrom. Martin is a Danish-born expert on marketing, culture, communication, user experience, and perhaps quite practically, common sense. Of the many books he's written, my all-time favorite is *Buyology: Truth and Lies About Why We Buy*, which is his genius take on how people make their purchasing decisions.

However, he wrote a subsequent book called *The Ministry of Common Sense*, where he talks about how easy it is for organizations to disconnect themselves from common sense, whether it be their culture, the truth about their products, the level to which their competition is eating their lunch, their position in the marketplace, their ability to reinvent themselves, or just confronting the brutal facts of where they are in connection with their customer. His book is phenomenal, and I highly recommend it.

In our interview, he discussed a laughable but shockingly common experience inside organizations that develops because of natural political silos, communication barriers, leaders with egos, and competing financial business goals.

No one tells this story better than Martin, so I invite you to read the transcript from our *On Leadership* interview about a seemingly arcane product-development process that arrogant leaders will laugh at and self-aware leaders will relate to.

SCOTT: Martin, you are, by most people's assessment, the world's leading expert on neuromarketing, on the reasons behind why people buy—which are sometimes counterintuitive. You've spent a lot of your recent years talking about and researching culture and congruency inside culture, why organizations do what they do, and where the points of hijack are.

Today, I'm going to toggle back and forth between your seminal book *Buyology* and your most recent book, well-named *The Ministry of Common Sense*. I think part of what makes you so influential is your ability to tell relatable stories that all of us can find ourselves in, much like I think Seth Godin—a friend of mine who has that same superpower.

One of the stories that you talk about is your experience inside a hotel room with the remote control—that anybody who's ever traveled has had an experience with. Would you take as much time as you need to tell that story? What are the lessons for anybody inside of an organization that has responsibility for marketing, communication, sales, product innovation, research, customer experience, user experience—what's the big insight?

MARTIN: My story began three years ago. I checked into a hotel in Miami, and I wanted to watch television. So, I grabbed my remote control (I actually stole it later on; I paid the hotel for it, by the way). It looked like a rocket ship. I wasn't sure if it was ready to take off, partly because it had two "on" buttons. I wasn't even sure how it worked.

So, I clicked away and managed to switch on the television after about five minutes. Then I watched television and I wanted to switch it off. And I couldn't. I'm not kidding, Scott. I could not switch off the television because the first off button—there were two—the first off button dimmed the light in the room in a kind of a moody, sexy way. When I clicked the second off button, guess what? The air-conditioning system and the minibar switched off, but my television was still running.

Of course, furious, at that point, I crawled under the bed with my butt in the air and unplugged all of this stuff. That really is my story. Except there's a part two that happened about a month later as I was on a plane to JFK. I was sitting next to this guy, and we were talking back and forth. At some point I asked him where he was from and he said, "Well, I'm from a small company. You've probably never heard about it."

I said, "Well, share with me." And guess what? The name he's saying is the name of that stupid remote control. And I said to him, "What the hell went wrong with you guys?"

Of course, this guy looked at me like a deer in the headlights, completely baffled about this passenger sitting next to him, now abusing him. So, he said, "What do you mean?"

I said, "Well, it's impossible to use your product. What went wrong?"

He said to me, "Listen, we actually had a problem internally in the old days. We had problems with the 'real estate.' We had the Netflix department, we had the TiVo area, we had the recording function, we had the TV, we had the radio function, the music, all that stuff; and each of those departments had all their different buttons they wanted to put on this remote control. Of course, it didn't have enough space." So, they managed to separate this into different zones. One zone was only TiVo, another one for Netflix, etc.

I said, "Yeah, but there's just one problem here. You have three numerical keyboards on this remote control."

He said, "Hold on, hold on. We had no conflicts whatsoever. It's been a smooth ride ever since. Everyone has what they want to have."

I said, "Except one thing—I don't know how to switch off your television."

This is really my point, because what I tend to see is that this is a little bit like a crack in the bridge, metaphorically speaking. If you have a company and you envision this as a big bridge, when you see this little crack on the side of the bridge, you know the foundation of that bridge is starting to collapse. Slowly collapse. What I've learned over the years is that when I looked at that remote control, it actually illustrated or exemplified a much bigger problem internally in the culture, a disconnect with the customers, a disconnect between the employees and the real world. And with that comes a lot of bureaucracy, a lack of common sense. With that, it becomes just a very contrived company.

So, at the end of the day, the remote control was a really good indication of the frustrations where companies have lost contact with who's paying the bill—which happens to be the customers.

Depending upon the nature of your career and the size of your organization, you may find this story to be a complete outlier, or a total validation of how often different business units fail to collaborate with the customers' end in mind. I can tell you from personal experience that no matter how well-intended, how well-educated, or how high the trust and collaboration is, there are always going to be self-serving challenges to achieve the results assigned to individual divisions. And so, the Transformational Insight from Martin Lindstrom I've titled Uncommon Sense is to recognize when you are caught in the common dilemma of speaking your language, serving your needs, focusing on your issues, as opposed to speaking the language of your client, meeting their needs, and solving their problems. And I think the nimblest, most agile, customer-focused organizations make it safe to raise those red flags, mid-development, midlaunch, or even prelaunch.

Recently, I had the privilege of interviewing Niren Chaudhary, the CEO of Panera Brands, on another podcast that I host for FranklinCovey called *C-suite conversations with Scott Miller*. One of the insights that I drew from this conversation with Niren was that whenever they're having an executive-level conversation inside Panera Brands, they don't leave the meeting until someone has dissented, not artificially, but as an expectation to see all sides of a debate. In the process, creating a culture in which everyone knows that dissent is safe at all levels. I think that's a remarkable attribute every leader should employ to ensure they're not designing the remote control for everyone but the end user: Martin Lindstrom in his hotel room.

Whatever your version of that remote control is, does it meet the needs of the end user? Sales, finance, marketing, supply chain, etc. all have needs. Martin's story demonstrates that even when everyone has a valid claim over their own real estate, it can leave the end user homeless. Beware of the leader who believes, at the surface level, everyone is aligned. Scratching a bit deeper may well reveal they may have budget or compensation incentives that are misaligned, and thus so is their end in mind. At the end of the day, the leader must be convinced that everyone is working with the same success factors in mind, and that their culture, strategy, systems, politics, and policies all align and support the same goal. This feels like a big *duh*, I know. But some Transformational

Insights are. Until they're brought to life through safe, transparent, collaborative, and vulnerable conversations where people are free to both dissent and bring common sense back into the culture. Hopefully, this won't require your organization setting up a formal Ministry of Common Sense but instead create an intentional culture where the person actually speaking common sense doesn't become the company pariah.

If you're not careful, you can end up with the product or service equivalent of the ill-designed remote control, where the only button the end user will care about is the one that turns you off—for good.

. . .

THE TRANSFORMATIONAL INSIGHT

Become hyperaware of the natural trap of well-intended, seemingly complementary (but perhaps misaligned or competing) people and divisions, and your overall culture ultimately hijacking your customers' experience.

THE QUESTION

Arthur Jones, sociologist and organizational design expert, said, "All organizations are perfectly aligned or designed to get the results they get." Do you have the courage to identify and call out the unnecessary and competing buttons on your "remote control"?

ALEX OSTERWALDER

FRANKLINCOVEY
ONLEADERSHIP
WITH SCOTT MILLER

EPISODE 141

ALEX OSTERWALDER
KNOWING THE BUSINESS
OF YOUR BUSINESS

WE ALL HAVE a series of defining moments in life that shape us, some perhaps more grandiose than others but memorable nonetheless in their impact.

Several of mine include:

- The late afternoon I completed my Florida licensed real estate exam and paid for the rapid results to see if I passed. Walked to my car alone. Ripped open the envelope and earned a 76. Passing was a 75. Maybe the greatest accomplishment of my life at age nineteen. Truly.

- Seeing Pope John Paul II deliver Good Friday Mass at the Colosseum in Rome.

- The day I opened my first Franklin Planner that my brother Mike bought and mailed me for my official career start at Disney (I recall which booth I was sitting in at Ronnie's

Restaurant in Orlando thirty years ago when I put it together. Interesting foreshadowing that I would someday become their CMO and invest 26+ years of my professional life with them).

- An evening in Greece sitting on a hotel balcony sharing a charcuterie board and champagne with my then girlfriend, now wife Stephanie, and our closest friends Chuck and Paula Farnsworth.

- The birth of our first son Thatcher. (Stephanie had natural childbirth with all three sons—not even an Advil, people—and it was traumatic . . . for me. Not for her. For me.)

And perhaps less important than all of these events (and many others) is an experience I had midcareer when I was serving as the leader of the central region sales division for FranklinCovey based in Chicago. Our company had just finished the design of a new multiday leadership solution and prior to a global launch we were certifying in the content all our leaders and dozens of our consultants who would soon be training our clients in it around the world.

About a hundred of us gathered in Orlando for a five-day certification program with the top talent of the organization. On day two, we began teaching the concept of building a leader's business acumen by understanding the five parts of business as designed by Ram Charan, the famed author and business consultant. Of his many books, we'd licensed the content from *What the CEO Wants You to Know*.

In this book, he illustrates what he calls the Five Parts of Business: Margin, Cash, Velocity, Customers, and Growth, and this was the concept we were all practicing that day.

Suddenly, an immensely competent consultant who specialized in leadership, culture, and all things organizational development, had this epiphany: he finally saw exactly how he fit into our company's business model and how his actions affected its success and profitability. As he was working through the Five Parts of Business, teaching it to a small group of us in a role-play, he and I came to realize his direct impact on FranklinCovey's money-making model. For the first time in his career with us, he became crystal clear on how his small decisions and behaviors could significantly and positively impact our company's profitability. It took this otherwise simple exercise around the Five Parts of Business for him to have a watershed experience about how certain things, well within his circle of control with clients, could disproportionately impact our profit and growth.

I suspect many haven't had that kind of epiphany connecting them and their work directly with what drives the enterprise.

Which begs the question: whether you're a leader of people or an individual contributor, how well do you know your organization's moneymaking model? Or as I like to say, the Business of Your Business

Further, if you are a leader, have you adequately explained it to everyone on your team so they intimately understand it and how their day-to-day decisions and contributions support it?

I suspect not. It's one of those things that gets lost in the whirlwind of day-to-day urgencies. Which makes Alex Osterwalder, Master Mentor #58, such a valuable addition to this volume.

I've been a raving fan of Alex through the entire *Strategyzer* series of books he's co-authored. The titles include *The Invincible Company*, *Value Proposition Design*, *Testing Business Ideas*, and *Business Model Generation*. Each of these books follows a strikingly impactful format, mainly paperback, landscape-oriented books that are highly illustrative and bring often complex business ideas and challenges to life visually for readers of all backgrounds and competencies. (Perhaps he knows David Sibbet, Master Mentor #54, or took one of his classes.)

I can't encourage you enough to check out the books he's co-authored, as they are invaluable in helping you understand some of the world's best thinking around innovation, design thinking, building enduring culture, and the Transformational Insight of this chapter, Knowing the Business of Your Business.

I ask again: how well do you Know the Business of Your Business? This question applies if you're the founder and owner, too. Do you clearly understand how you make money? And when I say money, I really mean profit. And are all your associates also clear on the Business of Your Business and how their daily actions build or destroy profit? Why should they care . . . ? Because profit is the lifeblood of every business and creates an organization that allows them to grow and learn and, minimally, earn a paycheck.

In his book *Business Model Generation*, Alex uses extraordinarily in-depth research to illustrate the business models of some of the strongest and most ensuring brands of our lifetimes, across a broad scope of industries. In essence, Alex is teaching the world the life or death need to intimately understand your organization's business model and to ensure every associate working with you not only knows it, but can clearly articulate how their daily decisions and behaviors are aligned to it. Or perhaps more importantly, misaligned.

Earlier in this chapter it might have seemed a stretch comparing seeing the Pope in person to watching a business colleague finally understand their connection to the company's business model. Both were memorable moments in my life, one personally and the other professionally. Watching my colleague's creativity unleash and confidence explode as he clearly understood his relevance and ability to impact our company's business model made me question how many of the other team members needed the same experience.

Alex's exhaustive illustration of some of the world's best business models should be a go-to resource for you as you're looking to fine-tune and clarify your own. If nothing less, Alex has brought to life that there are countless business models available to you. Finding the one that you perhaps can maximize better than anyone else, and clarifying its components to everyone in your organization, is an unmistakable business differentiator.

There's no more powerful momentum in business than clarity. Clarity on mission, purpose, contribution, values, customers, differentiation, the business landscape, and your value proposition. All of that, of course, doesn't matter if you're not making money since every organization has one of two purposes: either make money or provide a service. And last time I checked, the latter requires money also.

At the risk of patronizing you, I want to remind you that as the founder, owner, or leader, just because you think you're explaining things clearly doesn't mean anyone working with or for you possesses the same clarity. And for that matter, are you sure you're being clear? Are any of your passion projects (even if they were your original idea) no longer relevant and not positively contributing to your business model? And do you have the confidence and humility to surface and challenge them? Publicly?

I'm going to ask this question one more time: have you taken and invested the time to fully understand the Business of Your Business and ensure you yourself are hyperaligned to it? And then, does everyone inside the organization have a similar level of clarity? Regardless of your answers, everyone should have a vulnerable and transparent conversation with their leader on their alignment and what small or significant adjustments need to be made.

For anyone reading this who isn't a business owner or formal leader of people in your organization, be reminded of the piercingly insightful comment from a colleague of mine, "You're never in the room when your career is decided for you." Repeat that a few times and when you're insulted enough from it, you'll be able to take near complete control of your career because the last person to ever lose their job is the one who is most closely tied to the company's moneymaking model.

How close are you?

THE TRANSFORMATIONAL INSIGHT

It is incumbent on you, whether you're the leader or not, to understand your organization's business model and align your daily behaviors and decisions directly to it.

THE QUESTION

Do you Know the Business of Your Business? And if not, how could you possibly expect anyone else to?

KORY KOGON

FRANKLINCOVEY
ONLEADERSHIP
WITH SCOTT MILLER

EPISODE 26

KORY KOGON
BUSY AS A BADGE

Kory's a kick-ass-and-take-names kind of lady.

She's from New York and that East Coast talk-straight style ain't everyone's cup of tea. Except for those who respond well to it—which would be me. I'm an East Coast guy with a dash of southern style. But generally, Kory and I speak the same language.

Kory's also got serious chops when it comes to a broad swath of professional skills. She's the lead author of FranklinCovey's *Wall Street Journal* bestseller, *The 5 Choices to Extraordinary Productivity*, as well as the lead author of two additional books on project management and presentation skills. As a senior leader and consultant at FranklinCovey, Kory has a mastery of literally all our 30+ solutions, something maybe two or three other consultants globally could claim. She's either facilitated or presented all our different content areas in more than 25 countries for our company.

Of Kory's many areas of expertise, time management and productivity are her crown jewels. For over a decade, she has served as

FranklinCovey's thought leader on all things productivity-related. In this chapter I'd like to share what I think is a Transformational Insight Kory brings to the proverbial personal and professional table—that many of us wear "Busy" as a Badge. Even a badge of honor. More on that in a moment.

Kory, like me, has a bit of a silver tongue and, I suspect, also like me, is an outward processor, meaning she and I have very few unexpressed thoughts. We like to hear out loud what we're thinking, and then, once we've said it, truly determine if we believe it or not. You've met us. You've worked for us. You've led us. Perhaps, in fact, you are us. We drive introverts nutty and often have to remind ourselves to calibrate our ratio of think-to-say better. But, having shared that, Kory's got a few zingers that are piercingly profound. One in particular is, "Stop telling me how busy you are." I personally find this a bit offensive, but most truths that hit close to home are.

I'm the busiest person I know. And I'm constantly a bit embarrassed by it.

Kory's axiom is my personal reminder to hourly reassess why ... why am I so busy? Why is my day booked back-to-back every business day with an overflow that always dominates my weekends? What hole in my life am I trying to fill with nonstop meetings, obligations, proposals, projects, and promises? Why am I bouncing from commitment to commitment often every hour, if not every half hour? In a twelve-hour workday, which is my life, that's sometimes twenty-four different projects I'm working on simultaneously.

Welcome to my brand of lunacy which defies every principle of quality ever taught by the experts, Kory included.

I've given this a lot of thought and am still awash in being busy. Despite being embarrassed by it, I still wear it as a badge. Perhaps it's because I deeply crave someone's approval. And when I say someone, I mean, apparently, everyone. Why am I taking on so much? More money? More fame? More influence?

More security? More credibility? More options? More freedom? More choice?

But I'm not alone, am I?

Perhaps you wear Busy as a Badge as well. Researchers Silvia Bellezza, Neeru Paharia, and Anat Keinan found that busyness has now become the ultimate status symbol (in contrast to previous centuries, when leisure time signaled financial and social success). They write, "By telling others that we are busy and working all the time, we are implicitly suggesting that we are sought after, which enhances our perceived status."

I asked Kory about how this played out organizationally. Here's what she had to say:

SCOTT: I've heard you talk about this common conundrum that professionals face, which is this idea of productivity versus activity. Why do people get so caught up into a lot of activity, known as busyness, when the true goal we're searching for is productivity? Are there telltale signs of when we're caught up in the world of being busy, and maybe not being productively busy?

KORY: Saying things like "I do my best work under pressure" is one sign. And the idea of almost purposeful procrastination is another. People will wait on things because they're waiting for the buzz. When I ask people, "Why do you feel like you do your best work under pressure? Or why do you procrastinate?" I'll get all kinds of different reasons, when the truth is they're drug addicts. It's adrenaline, it's dopamine going to the reward center, creating that feeling. We know from studies that you cannot possibly do your best work at the last minute, but we feel that way.

SCOTT: About a decade ago, an oft-quoted article from the *Harvard Business Review* was titled, "Beware the Busy Manager." What are the risks of being the busy manager, the leader who's always in motion with lots of whirlwind, you might call them "Pigpen," if you will, of the workforce? What is the risk of working for or being that manager?

KORY: The risk is that everybody on your team feels like they have to do it the same way. They're going to leave you and find another company to work with. Because people can handle spurts of intense activity and intense pressure, but no one wants to work in a sustained culture of frenzy that might be giving the leader a perverted sense of validation. A manager like that got promoted because they did good work and they did a lot of work. They got the pat on the back and the recognition that got them into this management job. A lot of them never make the switch without help. They think, "I got promoted for doing all that stuff. I need to keep doing all of that. And the sign of me being a great manager is if I am busy all the time." The problem is that with people today, the badge of busyness is fading, is tarnishing. Busyness is going by the wayside.

SCOTT: What I hear you saying is that organizations are changing how they measure performance, away from activity and much more toward outcomes.

KORY: I don't know if the organization is, but people are putting the line in the sand around that. They want to be measured against outcomes, not by activity. That's why you have the Great Resignation.

SCOTT: I also hear you saying that if someone identifies as being a super busy manager, perhaps measuring their contribution through activity, that might actually not only be their fault. It might be a cultural imperative. They've been rewarded throughout their career, promoted, made more money, and told subconsciously, "Keep doing that. Keep doing that. Keep doing that." It's a cultural conundrum that organizations have to look at in its entirety. And not just the fact that someone loves frenzy.

KORY: Look at all the organizations that put Ping-Pong tables in, that brought dinner in, that made sure there were places to lie down overnight. Organizations built that culture of busy and made people compete against it, and it became a badge of honor if you stayed at the office twenty-four hours a day.

Whatever your personal reasons are, as Master Mentor #50 Joel Peterson (chapter twenty) likes to say, "There are no solutions, just trade-offs." So what are you accepting as your trade-off for all that busyness you've wrapped yourself in, and how can you become more proficient at making high value decisions on how you spend your time, energy, and attention?

Another adage from Kory reads like this: "The competitive edge for our new world of work will be held by those people, teams, and organizations that are consciously, intentionally, and methodically making the highest value decisions in the midst of unlimited choices and constant change."

So there are decisions and there are *high value decisions* all competing for our time and attention. Which seems simple enough—out of every possible option, make the *best* decision. "Says easy, does hard," as Dr. Covey would insert here. But the alternative is settling for busyness instead of true effectiveness.

. . .

THE TRANSFORMATIONAL INSIGHT

As Kory says, "Stop telling me how busy you are." Instead, reflect on whether you're getting the *right* things done.

THE QUESTION

Why do you use your busyness as a status symbol? How could you focus more on high value decisions instead?

ED MYLETT

FRANKLINCOVEY
ONLEADERSHIP
WITH SCOTT MILLER

EPISODE 101

ED MYLETT
WHAT'S YOUR KIT CAR?

I FIRST BECAME aware of Ed Mylett when I saw him present at Rachel and Dave Hollis's RISE Business event in Charleston, South Carolina, in November 2019. I was backstage in the green room with other speakers preparing for my appearance along with Marie Forleo, Chris Hogan, and Amy Porterfield. While I was watching Ed on the monitor bring a 7,000-person audience to tears (in a good way), I marveled at the hilarity, joy, laughter, introspection, and full range of emotions he pulled out of them. In my thirty-year conference history, his ability to build connection in an arena-sized setting was unprecedented. I was thinking, "Who is this guy?" Now truth be told, much of the world knew who Ed Mylett was, just not Scott Jeffrey Miller.

But at that moment, I became so wrapped up in his storytelling skills, I walked away from the networking opportunities in the green room and became transfixed, listening to one story in particular, which I asked Ed to re-create on our podcast. It is here in his own words. Ed remains to this day my favorite interview in more than 250 *On Leadership* podcast episodes.

SCOTT: Ed, when I think of your brand, I think of you as a master storyteller. As people have become more familiar with you on podcasts and interviews and on the speaking circuit around the nation, they recognize that as well.

I'd like you to take a few moments now and tell one of my favorite stories. It has to do with a Mercedes-Benz. I would love you to share it in detail—don't short-circuit it—because when I heard this story six months ago for the first time, I've thought about it ever since. I have told this story at countless dinner parties because I think the beauty of the message, beyond the humor, is how grounded you are today given your massive financial success. Your family is still together and healthy. And I think how you tell your stories with humility is such a treat. Please re-create the Mercedes-Benz story.

ED: First, before I tell you, it's true about the water being turned off as well. I don't think, had I not had those circumstances happen to me, that I would have been afforded some element of humility. In other words, I wasn't going down that track in my life. I was a guy who thought he was a pretty big deal when I was a baseball player, and I quickly learned I wasn't. And the Mercedes story is sort of reflective of that.

[Note from Scott: I implore you to watch or listen to the interview with Ed Mylett for greater context about his reference to the water being cut off in his apartment and he and his wife needing to shower poolside. It speaks so piercingly to his character and drive for success. Trust me. It's a must-listen.]

I wanted to be successful so badly, and I wanted to look successful so badly that I was willing to go to any measure to do it. So, I had a sales team at that time of people I was coaching to get into the financial industry.

I felt like I needed to look like I had a nice car so that I had some results, and I wanted a Mercedes. I wanted a 500SL convertible Mercedes, but I couldn't afford one.

I was thumbing through something called *The Pennysaver* back in the day, and they had a kit car Mercedes. Kit cars are typically not very good. Your normal kit car is a fake Mercedes and, in this case, a Chrysler LeBaron. They strip the body off of it—I'm not exaggerating—and they weld to the frame of that LeBaron a Mercedes body. It's a little bit too long, it doesn't quite fit, but you get the picture: on the outside is a Mercedes body; on the inside is a Chrysler LeBaron. They're very cheap and inexpensive. They weld these cars together so you can get one for almost nothing and they're sort of a joke.

I found one down in Laguna Beach. I drive down there (where I now live to this day), and I met a lady who had one. I think there was probably some methamphetamine involved in her life at that time. She was not on good times. And she's got this kit car, which is a joke. You get the picture. It's not quite the right size, except hers was even worse. I'm not exaggerating when I tell you this: this car was not welded together with a Mercedes body on a Chrysler LeBaron. It was Velcroed together. I'm not kidding you. This was a Velcroed-together car. So, it's an old beat-up Chrysler LeBaron Velcroed onto the frame of the car: a Mercedes body.

And I wanted it so bad.

So, I buy this thing from her. She warns me when I'm leaving, "Make sure when you slow down at a stoplight that you kind of ease into it because crazy things will happen."

Well, little did I know that the following scenario played out for me—this has happened to me more than a hundred times in my life, what I'm about to tell you.

Imagine me in my suit trying to look like a young professional dude in my fake Mercedes that almost everybody knows isn't a real one. I would roll up to a stoplight at an intersection, a busy intersection, but I'd stop a little bit too quickly, and the front headlight would fly off into the intersection. I would have to get out of my car and stop traffic both ways. All the cars are stopped. I'm stopping traffic. I'm in an intersection. I pick up my own headlight. I walk back and I stick it back on the Mercedes and I get back in my car again, humiliated as all these people are laughing.

If this was social media, I would be the most viral person in the history of social media. I've had that scenario, Scott, happen more than a hundred times, where I had to go and collect my own headlight and Velcro it back onto the car again because it was falling apart. Worse than that, if I got a little panicked and I shut the door too fast, the door would fall off the car and I would have to go out and pick up the door and Velcro it back on.

This culminated—I'm such a good liar—where, at that time, Chrysler and Mercedes merged and I walked back into my office after I bought the car. I said, "Hey, guys, I don't know if you've heard, but this new thing's coming out called a hybrid," which didn't exist at the time, "and it's a hybrid Mercedes and Chrysler and I got the first one in the world. It's a super cutting-edge, incredible car. I'm never going to have you ride on the inside of it but go take a look."

My guys are looking at it like, "This is very strange." On top of that, when you would ride in the car, the heater would blow the whole time. It was a beat up, wobbly Chrysler.

One day, we're at a sales conference. After all these humiliating experiences with Velcroing my car back together, we're at a sales retreat and we leave. My guys are all following me in their cars, back to the hotel.

Well, I get pulled over by the police and I'm wondering why they pulled me over. I was going the speed limit. So, I want you to picture my entire company's parked behind me right down the block, maybe one hundred yards away from me, twenty cars. The police come. Then another car; then another. Now there's four police cars. They make me stick my hands out the window. They handcuff me, put me in the back of a police car—haven't told me why I'm getting arrested—in front of my team.

Finally, I asked, "Sir, can you please tell me why I'm being arrested? You've read me my rights. I don't know what crime I've committed. I wasn't speeding."

He goes, "This is a stolen vehicle."

I go, "A stolen vehicle? Huh. Did I not file the title when I bought this thing?"

So, I'm back in the car about eight, ten more minutes and I go, "Oh my gosh, I wonder if they're running the plates on this car?" I said, "Officer, sir, why do you think the car's stolen?"

He goes, "The plates are stolen."

I said, "Sir, you're not going to believe what I'm about to tell you, but that's not a Mercedes-Benz that you're looking at. It's a Chrysler LeBaron, like the license plate says."

He goes, "What are you talking about?"

I said, "Sir, if you go up to my driver's side door and just pull on it, it's Velcroed on the vehicle."

The officer looks at me and he goes, "Is this turning into a DUI, boy?"

I said, "No, sir."

It's getting dark, so we got the lights on the car and the three police officers walk up and I pull my door off my own car. Pop! Pull it off, spin it, and throw it in the bushes, and all the police fall down in laughter.

And now my entire team is wondering, "What? His car's Velcroed together. This isn't a hybrid. He's been lying the whole time."

They finally put me back in the car. We drive back to the hotel. I'm such a good salesman, I sold that car that night to one of my own guys: "This thing's brought me a lot of luck."

So, the beginning of my business career, I drove a Velcroed-together car. I'm the only entrepreneur you will ever have on this show, brother, who can testify that he's driven a Velcroed car for two years of his life, trying to look like a big shot when he wasn't one. That definitely gives you humility, when you're going and picking up your own headlight and Velcroing it back on your car in front of hundreds of people.

I don't know about you, but every time I hear or read this story, I cry and laugh simultaneously.

In full transparency, I struggled with how I wanted to term this Transformational Insight from Ed, because I think everyone reading this will take something different away from it. I'm loath to even prescribe what the Transformational Insight could be for you, but because I listed the insights on the back cover of this book and in the table of contents, I'm forced to write something. Thus, I choose What's Your Kit Car? as Ed's Transformational Insight.

I have learned more from Ed Mylett than most people I've interviewed, and I'm in awe of his ability to turn his vulnerability into fuel for others. That takes not just confidence, but abundance. Some Transformational Insights are so applicable as to defy a prescriptive label. Ed's is a gift for everyone to take and make their own.

Your Transformational Insight might be different from another reader's. It could be around vulnerability, teaching through your messes, or imposter syndrome. This story might be validating to you at different points in your life. It might be that you just simply needed a hysterical story at the end of this book and I'm giving you one because you needed an uplift in life. You might have had a setback and you're trying to pivot forward. It may be that you've been masquerading as someone different than who you really are or need to be for yourself and others.

So choose your own insight and take the time to watch (not listen, but watch) Ed's entire interview. I think you will find it truly transformational while you determine What's Your Kit Car.

. . .

THE TRANSFORMATIONAL INSIGHT

If the metaphorical headlights fall off your car at the intersection, hold it high for all to see . . . and even learn from it.

THE QUESTION

What have you Velcroed over, hoping it doesn't fall off?

CONCLUSION

This book began with the transformational insight from Zafar Masud who miraculously survived a plane crash and shared the power of determining *What's Next?* in our lives. It ended with a hilarious and vulnerable story from Ed Mylett who knowingly bought the body of one car Velcroed onto the frame of another. One story with massive emotional weight and another with joyous levity. One completely unrelatable in terms of the actual event and one likely more relatable than we might care to admit. Bookends that hopefully leave you fulfilled and inspired to transform those areas in your life where you feel there's growth waiting to be tapped and unleashed.

Let's recap each of the thirty Master Mentors in *Volume 2*:

Zafar Masud—What's Next?
Bobby Herrera—Be a Transition Figure
Marie Forleo—Everything Is Figureoutable
Sean Covey—Self-Worth, Self-Esteem, and Self-Confidence
Tasha Eurich—Self-Awareness
Colin Cowie—The Gold Standard
Tiffany Aliche—There's No Such Thing as Overnight
    Success
Turia Pitt—Asking for and Accepting Help
BJ Fogg—Tiny Habits
Erica Dhawan—Be Intentional About Your Virtual Presence

Chester Elton—Anxiety in the Workplace
Julian Treasure—Listen to the Listening
Patty McCord—What Language Are You Speaking?
Greg Moore—Sharing the Journey
Madeline Levine—Self-Regulation
Jon Gordon—Tell the Truth Mondays
Patrick Bet-David—Your Future Truth
Rita McGrath—Seeing Around Corners
Geoffrey Moore—Crossing the Chasm
Joel Peterson—Entrepreneurial Leadership
Guy Kawasaki—A Buffet of Good Advice
Michael Hyatt—Your Productivity System
Julie Morgenstern—Time to Parent
David Sibbet—Visual Communication
Leena Rinne—Learn the Hidden Story
Jon Huntsman Jr.—Hard Work Still Matters
Martin Lindstrom—Uncommon Sense
Alex Osterwalder—Knowing the Business of Your Business
Kory Kogon—Busy as a Badge
Ed Mylett—What's Your Kit Car?

And since you're still with me, here is a recap of the first thirty Master Mentors from *Volume 1* and their Transformational Insights.

Nick Vujicic—Gratitude
Stephanie McMahon—Your Brand Is How You Show Up
Dave Hollis—Vulnerability
Susan David—Emotional Agility
Daniel Pink—Peak, Trough, and Recovery
Karen Dillon—Deliberate vs. Emergent Strategies
Anne Chow—What's Your Motive?
Chris McChesney—Keep a Compelling Scoreboard
Daniel Amen—Protect Your Brain

General Stanley McChrystal—Be on the Right Side
    of History
Kim Scott—Radical Candor
Dorie Clark—Twist If You Can't Invert (And Even If
    You Can)
Bob Whitman—The Servant Leader
Susan Cain—Rethinking Introverts and Extroverts
Ryan Holiday—Self-Discipline
Nely Galán—Hype Your Failures
Leif Babin—Extreme Ownership
Stedman Graham—Choose Your Identify
Liz Wiseman—Be a Multiplier and Not a Diminisher
Jay Papasan—The ONE Thing
Seth Godin—Fearless vs. Reckless
Todd Davis—The Power of Relationships
Donald Miller—Clarify Your Message
Michele Jessica Fièvre—Balancing Efficiency with
    Effectiveness
Whitney Johnson—Disrupt Yourself
Trent Shelton—The Power Perspective
Brendon Burchard—Prolific Quality Output
Stephen M. R. Covey—Pulling the Plug
Nancy Duarte—The PowerPoint Plague
Eric Barker—Knowing Your Story

I'm certain you didn't find all thirty chapters to be transformational for you—that's an impossible task for any author and wasn't my goal. Instead, my intention was to provide you with a curated buffet that might hit you exactly where you are in your life—perhaps at this very moment. Not to say every item on the metaphorical food line has the same relevance or appeal, but they very well could. Life rarely serves up the same dish twice.

As I mentioned in the introduction, it's no easy lift to shepherd thirty thought leaders and their ideas, while gaining their respective permissions and sign-offs, and then weave it all together into a single book. But for me, it's a labor of love. Don't forget, these are *my* mentors, too—drawn from different walks of life that I've had the privilege to interview and get to know. And if they've been included in this collection, it's because after diving into their stories, I found a desire to share them in as many ways possible. My hope is you've found enough Transformational Insights to turn *What's Next* from a question to a declaration. Go ahead and show the world *What's Next* for you.

As for me, *What's Next* means getting to work on *Master Mentors Volume 3*. That means thirty new Master Mentors including Mel Robbins, Emmanuel Acho, Grant Cardone, and Deepak Chopra . . . just to name a few. Hope to see you there.

INDEX

ABOUT THE AUTHOR

SCOTT JEFFREY MILLER is a highly sought-after speaker, author, podcast host, and podcast guest. He has authored six books, including *Wall Street Journal* and #1 Amazon New Release bestsellers. Scott currently serves as FranklinCovey's senior advisor on thought leadership, leading the strategy and development of the firm's speakers bureau, as well as the publication of podcasts, webcasts, and bestselling books. Prior to his advisor role, Scott was a twenty-five-year FranklinCovey associate, serving as the chief marketing officer and executive vice president of business development. Scott hosts *On Leadership with Scott Miller*, the world's largest weekly leadership podcast.

MASTER MENTORS
VOLUME 1

Now that you've finished *Master Mentors Volume 2,* pick up a copy of *Master Mentors Volume 1,* which debuted as an Amazon #1 New Release in Business Mentoring and Coaching.

Highlighting major celebrities and luminaries to less well-known but equally brilliant and influential minds, this book is an easy-to-read and practical guide on how to implement these 30 transformative insights into your own life.

#1 Amazon New Release

--- **ORDER FROM YOUR FAVORITE RETAILER TODAY** ---

amazon BARNES &NOBLE   INDIEBOUND.org   bookpal   BAM! BOOKS-A-MILLION

30 MASTER MENTORS

Nick Vujicic	Daniel Amen	Nely Galán	Michele Jessica Fièvre
Stephanie McMahon	General Stanley McChrystal	Leif Babin	Whitney Johnson
Dave Hollis	Kim Scott	Stedman Graham	Trent Shelton
Susan David	Dorie Clark	Liz Wiseman	Brendon Burchard
Daniel Pink	Bob Whitman	Jay Papasan	Stephen M. R. Covey
Karen Dillon	Susan Cain	Seth Godin	Nancy Duarte
Anne Chow	Ryan Holiday	Todd Davis	Eric Barker
Chris McChesney		Donald Miller	

SCHEDULE
SCOTT MILLER
TO SPEAK AT YOUR NEXT EVENT

Are you planning an event for your organization? Schedule Scott Miller to deliver an engaging keynote speech tailored to your leaders or audience.

- Association and Industry Conferences
- Sales Conferences
- Annual Meetings
- Leadership Developments

- Executive and Board Retreats
- Company Functions
- Onsite Consulting
- Client Engagements

Scott Miller has spoken at hundreds of conferences and client events worldwide and is the host of the FranklinCovey-sponsored webcast, podcast *On Leadership with Scott Miller.*

To schedule Scott Miller today, call
1-888-554-1776
or visit franklincovey.com.

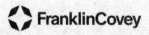

FranklinCovey

FranklinCovey is the most trusted leadership company in the world, with operations in over 160 countries. We transform organizations by partnering with our clients to build leaders, teams, and cultures that get breakthrough results through collective action, which leads to a more engaging work experience for their people.

Available through the FranklinCovey All Access Pass®, our best-in-class content, solutions, experts, technology, and metrics seamlessly integrate to ensure lasting behavior change at scale.

This approach to leadership and organizational change has been tested and refined by working with tens of thousands of teams and organizations over the past 30 years.

To learn more, visit
FRANKLINCOVEY.COM.

The FranklinCovey All Access Pass® provides unlimited access to our best-in-class content and solutions, allowing you to expand your reach, achieve your business objectives, and sustainably impact performance across your organization.

AS A PASSHOLDER, YOU CAN:

- Access FranklinCovey's world-class content, whenever and wherever you need it, including *The 7 Habits of Highly Effective People®: Signature Edition 4.0*, Leading at the *Speed of Trust®*, *The 5 Choices to Extraordinary Productivity®*, and *Unconscious Bias: Understanding Bias to Unleash Potential™*.

- Certify your internal facilitators to teach our content, deploy FranklinCovey consultants, or use digital content to reach your learners with the behavior-changing content you require.

- Have access to a certified implementation specialist who will help design Impact Journeys for behavior change.

- Organize FranklinCovey content around your specific business-related needs.

- Build a common learning experience throughout your entire global organization with our core-content areas localized into 23 languages.

Join thousands of organizations using the All Access Pass to implement strategy, close operational gaps, increase sales, drive customer loyalty, and improve employee engagement.

To learn more, visit
FRANKLINCOVEY.COM or call **1-888-868-1776**.

FRANKLINCOVEY
ONLEADERSHIP
WITH
SCOTT MILLER

Join *On Leadership* host Scott Miller for weekly interviews with thought leaders, bestselling authors, and world-renowned experts on the topics of organizational culture, leadership development, execution, and personal productivity.

FEATURED INTERVIEWS INCLUDE:

CHRIS McCHESNEY
THE 4 DISCIPLINES OF EXECUTION

SUSAN DAVID
EMOTIONAL AGILITY

KIM SCOTT
RADICAL CANDOR

DANIEL PINK
WHEN

SETH GODIN
THE DIP, LINCHPIN, PURPLE COW

NELY GALÁN
SELF MADE

LIZ WISEMAN
MULTIPLIERS / IMPACT PLAYERS

GUY KAWASAKI
WISE GUY

STEPHEN M. R. COVEY
THE SPEED OF TRUST

ARIANNA HUFFINGTON
THRIVE NOW

NANCY DUARTE
DATA STORY, SLIDE:OLOGY

STEPHANIE McMAHON
CEO, WWE

DEEPAK CHOPRA
ABUNDANCE

ANNE CHOW
CEO, AT&T BUSINESS

GENERAL STANLEY McCHRYSTAL
LEADERS: MYTH AND REALITY

MATTHEW McCONAUGHEY
GREENLIGHTS

Subscribe to FranklinCovey's *On Leadership podcast* to receive weekly videos, tools, and articles.

FRANKLINCOVEY.COM/ONLEADERSHIP.

READ MORE
FROM THE FRANKLINCOVEY LIBRARY

MORE THAN 50 MILLION COPIES SOLD

Learn more about how to develop yourself personally, lead your team,
or transform your organization with these bestselling books, by visiting
7habitsstore.com.